Abraham Lincoln, George Washington

The Ideals of the Republic

Or, great words from great Americans

Abraham Lincoln, George Washington

The Ideals of the Republic
Or, great words from great Americans

ISBN/EAN: 9783337038014

Printed in Europe, USA, Canada, Australia, Japan

Cover: Foto ©Suzi / pixelio.de

More available books at **www.hansebooks.com**

THE

IDEALS OF THE REPUBLIC

OR

GREAT WORDS FROM GREAT AMERICANS

NEW YORK AND LONDON

G. P. PUTNAM'S SONS

The Knickerbocker Press

The Knickerbocker Press, New York
Electrotyped, Printed, and Bound by
G. P. Putnam's Sons

CONTENTS.

THE DECLARATION OF INDE-PENDENCE

THE DECLARATION OF INDE-
PENDENCE.*

In Congress, July 4, 1776.
By the Representatives of the United States in Congress assembled.

A DECLARATION.

WHEN, in the course of human events, it becomes necessary for one people to dissolve the political bands which have connected them with another, and to assume among the powers of the earth the separate and equal station to which the laws of nature and of nature's God entitle them, a decent respect for the opinions of mankind requires that they should declare the causes which impel them to the separation.

* See Appendix, page 191.

We hold these truths to be self-evident :
—that all men are created equal ; that
they are endowed by their Creator with
certain unalienable rights ; that among
these are life, liberty, and the pursuit of
happiness ; that, to secure these rights,
governments are instituted among men,
deriving their just powers from the consent of the governed ; that whenever any
form of government becomes destructive
of these ends it is the right of the people
to alter or to abolish it, and to institute a
new government, laying its foundation
on such principles, and organizing its
powers in such form, as to them shall
seem most likely to effect their safety and
happiness.   Prudence, indeed, will dictate that governments long established
should not be changed for light and
transient causes ; and accordingly all experience hath shown that mankind are
more disposed to suffer, while evils are
sufferable, than to right themselves by
abolishing the forms to which they are
accustomed.   But when a long train of

abuses and usurpations, pursuing invari-
ably the same object, evinces a design to
reduce them under absolute despotism, it
is their right, it is their duty, to throw off
such government, and to provide new
guards for their future security. Such
has been the patient sufferance of these
colonies ; and such is now the necessity
which constrains them to alter their
former system of government. The history of the present king of Great Britain
is a history of repeated injuries and usurpations, all having in direct object the
establishment of an absolute tyranny over
these states. To prove this, let facts be
submitted to a candid world.

He has refused his assent to laws the
most wholesome and necessary for the
public good.

He has forbidden his governors to pass
laws of immediate and pressing importance, unless suspended in their operation
till his assent should be obtained ; and,
when so suspended, he has utterly neg-
lected to attend to them.

He has refused to pass other laws for the accommodation of large districts of people, unless those people would relinquish the right of representation in the legislature—a right inestimable to them, and formidable to tyrants only.

He has called together legislative bodies at places unusual, uncomfortable, and distant from the depository of their public records, for the sole purpose of fatiguing them into compliance with his measures.

He has dissolved representative houses repeatedly, for opposing, with manly firmness, his invasions on the rights of the people.

He has refused, for a long time after such dissolutions, to cause others to be elected ; whereby the legislative powers, incapable of annihilation, have returned to the people at large for their exercise ; the state remaining, in the meantime, exposed to all the danger of invasion from without and convulsions within.

He has endeavored to prevent the population of these states ; for that purpose obstructing the laws for naturalization of foreigners, refusing to pass others to encourage their migration hither, and raising the conditions of new appropriations of lands.

He has obstructed the administration of justice, by refusing his assent to laws for establishing judiciary powers.

He has made judges dependent on his will alone for the tenure of their offices and the amount and payment of their salaries.

He has erected a multitude of new offices, and sent hither swarms of officers, to harass our people and eat out their substance.

He has kept among us, in times of peace, standing armies, without the consent of our legislatures.

He has affected to render the military independent of and superior to the civil power.

He has combined with others to subject us to a jurisdiction foreign to our constitution and unacknowledged by our laws;

giving his assent to their acts of pretended legislation,—

For quartering large bodies of armed troops among us :

For protecting them, by a mock trial, from punishment for any murders which they should commit on the inhabitants of these states :

For cutting off our trade with all parts of the world :

For imposing taxes on us without our consent :

For depriving us, in many cases, of the benefits of trial by jury :

For transporting us beyond seas, to be tried for pretended offences :

For abolishing the free system of English law in a neighboring province, establishing therein an arbitrary government, and enlarging its boundaries so as to render it at once an example and fit instrument for introducing the same absolute rule into these colonies :

For taking away our charters, abolishing our most valuable laws, and altering fundamentally the forms of our government :

For suspending our own legislatures, and declaring themselves invested with power to legislate for us in all cases whatsoever.

He has abdicated government here by declaring us out of his protection, and waging war against us.

He has plundered our seas, ravaged our coasts, burned our towns, and destroyed the lives of our people.

He is at this time transporting large armies of foreign mercenaries, to complete the works of death, desolation, and tyranny, already begun, with circumstances of cruelty and perfidy scarcely paralleled in the most barbarous ages, and totally unworthy the head of a civilized nation.

He has constrained our fellow-citizens, taken captive on the high seas, to bear arms against their country, to become the executioners of their friends and brethren, or to fall themselves by their hands.

He has excited domestic insurrections

amongst us, and has endeavored to bring on the inhabitants of our frontiers the merciless Indian savages, whose known rule of warfare is an undistinguished destruction of all ages, sexes, and conditions.

In every stage of these oppressions we have petitioned for redress in the most humble terms; our petitions have been answered only by repeated injury. A prince whose character is thus marked by every act which may define a tyrant is unfit to be the ruler of a free people.

Nor have we been wanting in attention to our British brethren. We have warned them, from time to time, of attempts made by their legislature to extend an unwarrantable jurisdiction over us. We have reminded them of the circumstances of our emigration and settlement here. We have appealed to their native justice and magnanimity, and we have conjured them, by the ties of our common kindred, to disavow these usurpations, which would inevitably interrupt our connections and correspondence. They, too, have been deaf to the voice of justice and consanguinity. We must therefore acquiesce in the necessity which denounces our separation, and hold them, as we hold the rest of mankind, enemies in war —in peace, friends.

We, therefore, the representatives of the United States of America, in General Congress assembled, appealing to the Supreme Judge of the world for the rectitude of our intentions, do, in the name and by the authority of the good people of these colonies, solemnly publish and declare that these United Colonies are, and of right ought to be, free and independent states ; that they are absolved from all allegiance to the British crown, and that all political connection between them and the state of Great Britain is, and ought to be, totally dissolved ; and that, as free and independent states, they have full power to levy war, conclude peace, contract alliances, establish commerce, and to do all other acts and things which independent states may of right do. And for the support of this declaration, with a firm reliance on the protection of Divine Providence, we mutually pledge to each other our lives, our fortunes, and our sacred honor.

Signed by order and in behalf of the Congress.

JOHN HANCOCK, President.

Attested, CHARLES THOMPSON, Secretary.

NEW HAMPSHIRE.

Josiah Bartlett,
William Whipple,
Matthew Thornton.

MASSACHUSETTS BAY.

Samuel Adams,
John Adams,
Robert Treat Paine,
Elbridge Gerry.

RHODE ISLAND, &c.

Stephen Hopkins,
William Ellery.

NEW JERSEY.

Richard Stockton,
John Witherspoon,
Francis Hopkinson,
John Hart,
Abraham Clark.

PENNSYLVANIA.

Robert Morris,
Benjamin Rush,
Benjamin Franklin,
John Morton,
George Clymer,
James Smith,
George Taylor,
James Wilson,
George Ross.

CONNECTICUT.

Roger Sherman,
Samuel Huntington,
William Williams,
Oliver Wolcott.

NEW YORK.

William Floyd,
Philip Livingston,
Francis Lewis,
Lewis Morris.

VIRGINIA.

George Wythe,
Richard Henry Lee,
Thomas Jefferson,
Benjamin Harrison,
Thomas Nelson, Jr.,
Francis Lightfoot Lee,
Carter Braxton.

NORTH CAROLINA.

William Hooper,
Joseph Hewes,
John Penn.

DELAWARE.

Cæsar Rodney,
George Read,
Thomas M'Kean.

MARYLAND.

Samuel Chase,
William Paca,
Thomas Stone,
Charles Carroll, of Carrollton.

SOUTH CAROLINA.

Edward Rutledge,
Thomas Heyward, Jr.,
Thomas Lynch, Jr.,
Arthur Middleton.

GEORGIA.

Button Gwinnett,
Lyman Hall,
George Walton.

CONSTITUTION OF THE UNITED STATES

CONSTITUTION OF THE UNITED STATES.*

WE the people of the United States, in order to form a more perfect union, establish justice, insure domestic tranquillity, provide for the common defence,

* The Constitution of the United States was adopted by a convention of the several States September 17, 1787. It was ratified by the States as follows : Delaware, December 7, 1787; Pennsylvania, December 12, 1787; New Jersey, December 18, 1787; Georgia, January 2, 1788; Connecticut, January 9, 1788; Massachusetts, February 6, 1788; Maryland, April 28, 1788; South Carolina, May 23, 1788; New Hampshire, June 21, 1788 ; Virginia, June 26, 1788 ; and New York, July 26, 1788.

Thus, on the 4th of March, 1789, the day fixed for commencing the operations of government under the new Constitution, it had been ratified by more than the required number of States.

North Carolina ratified it November 21, 1789; Rhode Island, on May 29, 1790; and Vermont, on January 10, 1791.

* See Appendix, page 192

promote the general welfare, and secure the blessings of liberty to ourselves and our posterity, do ordain and establish this Constitution for the United States of America.

ARTICLE I.

Section 1. All legislative powers herein granted shall be vested in a Congress of the United States, which shall consist of a Senate and a House of Representatives.

Sec. 2. The House of Representatives shall be composed of members chosen every second year by the people of the several States, and the electors in each State shall have the qualifications requisite for electors of the most numerous branch of the State legislature.

No person shall be a Representative who shall not have attained the age of twenty-five years, and been seven years a citizen of the United States, and who shall not, when elected, be an inhabitant of that State in which he shall be chosen.

[Representatives and direct taxes shall be apportioned among the several States which may be included within this Union, according to their respective numbers, which shall be determined by adding to the whole number of free persons, including those bound to service for a term of years, and excluding Indians not taxed, three fifths of all other persons.]* The actual enumeration shall be made within three years after the first meeting of the Congress of the United States, and within every subsequent term of ten years, in such manner as they shall by law direct. The number of Representatives shall not exceed one for every thirty thousand, but each State shall have at least one Representative ; and until such enumeration shall be made, the State of New Hampshire shall be entitled to choose three, Massachusetts eight, Rhode Island and Providence Plantations one, Connecticut five, New York six, New Jersey four,

* The clause included in brackets is amended by the XIVth Amendment, 2d section.

Pennsylvania eight, Delaware one, Maryland six, Virginia ten, North Carolina five, South Carolina five, and Georgia three.

When vacancies happen in the representation from any State, the executive authority thereof shall issue writs of election to fill such vacancies.

The House of Representatives shall choose their speaker and other officers; and shall have the sole power of impeachment.

Sec. 3. The Senate of the United States shall be composed of two Senators from each State, chosen by the legislature thereof, for six years; and each Senator shall have one vote.

Immediately after they shall be assembled in consequence of the first election, they shall be divided as equally as may be into three classes. The seats of the Senators of the first class shall be vacated at the expiration of the second year, of the second class at the expiration of the fourth year, and of the third class, at the expiration of the sixth year, so that one third may be chosen every second year; and if vacancies happen by resignation, or otherwise, during the recess of the legislature of any State, the executive thereof may make temporary appointments until the next meeting of the legislature, which shall then fill such vacancies.

No person shall be a Senator who shall not have attained to the age of thirty years, and been nine years a citizen of the United States, and who shall not, when elected, be an inhabitant of that State for which he shall be chosen.

The Vice-President of the United States shall be President of the Senate, but shall have no vote, unless they be equally divided.

The Senate shall choose their other officers, and also a President *pro tempore*, in the absence of the Vice-President, or when he shall exercise the office of President of the United States.

The Senate shall have sole power to

try all impeachments. When sitting for that purpose, they shall be on oath or affirmation. When the President of the United States is tried, the Chief Justice shall preside; and no person shall be convicted without the concurrence of two thirds of the members present.

Judgment in cases of impeachment shall not extend further than to removal from office, and disqualification to hold and enjoy any office of honor, trust, or profit under the United States; but the party convicted shall nevertheless be liable and subject to indictment, trial, judgment, and punishment, according to law.

Sec. 4. The times, places, and manner of holding elections for Senators and Representatives shall be prescribed in each State by the legislature thereof; but the Congress may at any time by law make or alter such regulations, except as to the places of choosing Senators.

The Congress shall assemble at least once in every year, and such meeting shall be on the first Monday in December, unless they shall by law appoint a different day.

Sec. 5. Each house shall be the judge of the elections, returns, and qualifications of its own members, and a majority of each shall constitute a quorum to do business ; but a smaller number may adjourn from day to day, and may be authorized to compel the attendance of absent members, in such manner and under such penalties as each house may provide.

Each house may determine the rules of its proceedings, punish its members for disorderly behavior, and, with the concurrence of two thirds, expel a member.

Each house shall keep a journal of its proceedings, and from time to time publish the same, excepting such parts as may in their judgment require secrecy ; and the yeas and nays of the members of either house on any question shall, at the desire of one fifth of those present, be entered on the journal.

Neither house, during the session of

Congress, shall, without the consent of the other, adjourn for more than three days, nor to any other place than that in which the two houses shall be sitting.

Sec. 6. The Senators and Representatives shall receive a compensation for their services, to be ascertained by law, and paid out of the Treasury of the United States. They shall in all cases, except treason, felony, and breach of the peace, be privileged from arrest during their attendance at the session of their respective houses, and in going to and returning from the same ; and for any speech or debate in either house, they shall not be questioned in any other place.

No Senator or Representative shall, during the time for which he was elected, be appointed to any civil office under the authority of the United States, which shall have been created, or the emoluments whereof shall have been increased, during such time ; and no person holding any office under the United States shall be a member of either house during his continuance in office.

Sec. 7. All bills for raising revenue shall originate in the House of Representatives ; but the Senate may propose or concur with amendments as on other bills.

Every bill which shall have passed the House of Representatives and the Senate, shall, before it becomes a law, be presented to the President of the United States ; if he approve he shall sign it, but if not he shall return it, with his objections to that house in which it shall have originated, who shall enter the objections at large on their journal, and proceed to reconsider it. If after such reconsideration two thirds of that house shall agree to pass the bill, it shall be sent, together with the objections, to the other house, by which it shall likewise be reconsidered, and if approved by two thirds of that house, it shall become a law. But in all cases the votes of both houses shall be determined by yeas and nays, and the names of the persons voting for and against the bill shall be entered on the journal of each house respectively. If any bill shall not be returned by the President within ten days (Sundays excepted) after it shall have been presented to him, the same shall be a law, in like manner as if he had signed it, unless the Congress by their adjournment prevent its return, in which case it shall not be a law.

Every order, resolution, or vote to which the concurrence of the Senate and the House of Representatives may be necessary (except on a question of adjournment) shall be presented by the President of the United States ; and before the same shall take effect, shall be approved by him, or being disapproved by him, shall be repassed by two thirds of the Senate and House of Representatives, according to the rules and limitations prescribed in the case of a bill.

Sec. 8. The Congress shall have power to lay and collect taxes, duties, imposts, and excises, to pay the debts and provide for the common defence and general welfare of the United States ; but all duties, imposts, and excises shall be uniform throughout the United States ;

To borrow money on the credit of the United States ;

To regulate commerce with foreign nations, and among the several States, and with the Indian tribes ;

To establish an uniform rule of naturalization, and uniform laws on the subject of bankruptcies throughout the United States ;

To coin money, regulate the value thereof, and of foreign coin, and fix the standard of weights and measures ;

To provide for the punishment of counterfeiting the securities and current coin of the United States ;

To establish post-offices and post-roads ;

To promote the progress of science and useful arts, by securing for limited times to authors and inventors the exclusive right to their respective writings and discoveries ;

To constitute tribunals inferior to the Supreme Court;

To define and punish piracies and felonies committed on the high seas, and offences against the law of nations;

To declare war, grant letters of marque and reprisal, and make rules concerning captures on land and water;

To raise and support armies, but no appropriation of money to that use shall be for a longer term than two years;

To provide and maintain a navy;

To make rules for the government and regulation of the land and naval forces;

To provide for calling forth the militia to execute the laws of the Union, suppress insurrections, and repel invasions;

To provide for organizing, arming, and disciplining the militia, and for governing such part of them as may be employed in the service of the United States, reserving to the States respectively the appointment of the officers, and the authority of training the militia according to the discipline prescribed by Congress;

To exercise exclusive legislation in all cases whatsoever, over such district (not exceeding ten miles square) as may, by cession of particular States, and the acceptance of Congress, become the seat of the Government of the United States, and to exercise like authority over all places purchased by the consent of the legislature of the State in which the same shall be, for the erection of forts, magazines, arsenals, dock-yards, and other needful buildings ; and

To make all laws which shall be necessary and proper for carrying into execution the foregoing powers, and all other powers vested by this Constitution in the Government of the United States, or in any department or officer thereof.

Sec. 9. The migration or importation of such persons as any of the States now existing shall think proper to admit, shall not be prohibited by the Congress prior to the year one thousand eight hundred and eight, but a tax or duty may be imposed on such importation, not exceeding ten dollars for each person.

The privilege of the writ of habeas corpus shall not be suspended, unless when in cases of rebellion or invasion the public safety may require it. .

No bill of attainder or *ex-post-facto* law shall be passed.

No capitation, or other direct tax shall be laid, unless in proportion to the census or enumeration hereinbefore directed to be taken.

No tax or duty shall be laid on articles exported from any State.

No preference shall be given by any regulation of commerce or revenue to the ports of one State over those of another : nor shall vessels bound to, or from, one State, be obliged to enter, clear, or pay duties in another.

No money shall be drawn from the Treasury, but in consequence of appropriations made by law ; and a regular statement and account of the receipts and the expenditures of all public money shall be published from time to time.

No title of nobility shall be granted by

the United States ; and no person holding any office of profit or trust under them shall, without the consent of the Congress, accept of any present, emolument, office, or title, of any kind whatever, from any king, prince, or foreign state.

Sec. 10. No State shall enter into any treaty, alliance, or confederation ; grant letters of marque and reprisal ; coin money ; emit bills of credit ; make any thing but gold and silver coin a tender in payment of debts ; pass any bill of attainder, *ex-post-facto* law, or law impairing the obligation of contracts, or grant any title of nobility.

No State shall, without the consent of Congress, lay any imposts or duties on imports or exports, except what may be absolutely necessary for executing its inspection laws ; and the net produce of all duties and imposts, laid by any State on imports or exports, shall be for the use of the Treasury of the United States ; and all such laws shall be subject to the revision and control of the Congress.

No State shall, without the consent of Congress, lay any duty of tonnage, keep troops, or ships of war in time of peace, enter into any agreement or compact with another State, or with a foreign power, or engage in war, unless actually invaded, or in such imminent danger as will not admit of delay.

ARTICLE II.

Section 1. The executive power shall be vested in a President of the United States of America. He shall hold his office during the term of four years, and, together with the Vice-President, chosen for the same term, be elected as follows :

Each State shall appoint, in such manner as the legislature thereof may direct, a number of electors, equal to the whole number of Senators and Representatives to which the State may be entitled in the Congress ; but no Senator or Representative, or person holding an office of trust or profit under the United States, shall be appointed an elector.

[The electors shall meet in their respective States, and vote by ballot for two persons, of whom one at least shall not be an inhabitant of the same State with themselves. And they shall make a list of all the persons voted for, and of the number of votes for each ; which list they shall sign and certify, and transmit sealed to the seat of the Government of the United States, directed to the President of the Senate. The President of the Senate shall, in the presence of the Senate and the House of Representatives, open all the certificates, and the votes shall then be counted. The person having the greatest number of votes shall be the President, if such number be a majority of the whole number of electors appointed ; and if there be more than one who have such majority, and have an equal number of votes, then the House of Representatives shall immediately choose by ballot one of them for President ; and if no person have a majority, then from the five highest on the list the said House shall in like manner choose the President. But in choosing the President, the votes shall be taken by States, the representation from each State having one vote ; a quorum for this purpose shall consist of a member or members from two thirds of the States, and a majority of all the States shall be necessary to a choice. In every case, after the choice of the President, the person having the greatest number of votes of the electors shall be the Vice-President. But if there should remain two or more who have equal votes, the Senate shall choose from them by ballot the Vice-President.]*

The Congress may determine the time of choosing the electors, and the day on which they shall give their votes ; which day shall be the same throughout the United States.

No person except a natural-born citizen, or a citizen of the United States, at the time of the adoption of this Constitution,

* This clause in brackets has been superseded by the XIIth Amendment.

shall be eligible to the office of President ; neither shall any person be eligible to that office who shall not have attained the age of thirty-five years, and been fourteen years a resident within the United States.

In case of the removal of the President from office, or of his death, resignation, or inability to discharge the powers and duties of the said office, the same shall devolve on the Vice-President, and the Congress may by law provide for the case of removal, death, resignation, or inability, both of the President and Vice-President, declaring what officer shall then act as President, and such officer shall act accordingly, until the disability be removed, or a President shall be elected.

The President shall, at stated times, receive for his services a compensation, which shall neither be increased nor diminished during the period for which he shall have been elected, and he shall not receive within that period any other emolument from the United States, or any of them.

Before he enter on the execution of his office, he shall take the following oath or affirmation :

"I do solemnly swear (or affirm) that I will faithfully execute the office of President of the United States, and will to the best of my ability, preserve, protect, and defend the Constitution of the United States."

Sec. 2. The President shall be Commander-in-Chief of the Army and Navy of the United States, and of the militia of the several States, when called into the actual service of the United States ; he may require the opinion, in writing, of the principal officer in each of the executive departments, upon any subject relating to the duties of their respective offices, and he shall have power to grant reprieves and pardons for offences against the United States, except in cases of impeachment.

He shall have power, by and with the advice and consent of the Senate, to make treaties, provided two thirds of the Senators present concur ; and he shall nominate, and by and with the advice and consent of the Senate, shall appoint ambassadors, other public ministers and consuls, judges of the Supreme Court, and all other officers of the United States, whose appointments are not herein otherwise provided for, and which shall be established by law ; but the Congress may by law vest the appointment of such inferior officers as they think proper, in the President alone, in the courts of laws, or in the heads of departments.

The President shall have power to fill up all vacancies that may happen during the recess of the Senate, by granting commissions which shall expire at the end of their next session.

Sec. 3. He shall from time to time give to the Congress information of the state of the Union, and recommend to their consideration such measures as he shall judge necessary and expedient ; he may, on extraordinary occasions, convene both houses, or either of them, and in case of disagreement between them, with respect to the time of adjournment, he may adjourn them to such time as he shall think proper ; he shall receive ambassadors and other public ministers ; he shall take care that the laws be faithfully executed, and shall commission all the officers of the United States.

Sec. 4. The President, Vice-President, and all civil officers of the United States, shall be removed from office on impeachment for, and conviction of, treason, bribery, or other high crimes and misdemeanors.

ARTICLE III.

Section 1. The judicial power of the United States, shall be vested in one Supreme Court, and in such inferior courts as the Congress may from time to time ordain and establish. The judges, both of the Supreme and inferior courts, shall hold their offices during good behavior, and shall, at stated times, receive for their services a compensation, which shall not be diminished during their continuance in office.

Sec. 2. The judicial power shall extend to all cases, in law and equity, arising under this Constitution, the laws of the United States, and treaties made, or which shall be made, under their authority ; to all cases affecting ambassadors, other public ministers, and consuls ; to all cases of admiralty and maritime jurisdiction ; to controversies to which the United States shall be a party ; to controversies between two or more States ; between a State and citizens of another State ; between citizens of different States ; between citizens of the same State claiming lands under grants of different States ; and between a State, or the citizens thereof, and foreign states, citizens, or subjects.

In all cases affecting ambassadors, other public ministers, and consuls, and those in which a State shall be a party, the Supreme Court shall have original jurisdiction. In all the other cases before mentioned, the Supreme Court shall have appellate jurisdiction, both as to law and fact, with such exceptions and under such regulations as the Congress shall make.

The trial of all crimes, except in cases of impeachment, shall be by jury ; and such trial shall be held in the State where the said crimes shall have been committed ; but when not committed within any State, the trial shall be at such place or places as the Congress may by law have directed.

Sec. 3. Treason against the United States shall consist only in levying war against them, or in adhering to their enemies, giving them aid and comfort. No person shall be convicted of treason unless on the testimony of two witnesses to the same overt act, or on confession in open court.

The Congress shall have power to declare the punishment of treason, but no attainder of treason shall work corruption of blood, or forfeiture, except during the life of the person attainted.

ARTICLE IV.

Section 1. Full faith and credit shall be given in each State to the public acts, records, and judicial proceedings of every other State. And the Congress may by general laws prescribe the manner in which such acts, records, and proceedings shall be proved, and the effect thereof.

Sec. 2. The citizens of each State shall be entitled to all privileges and immunities of citizens in the several States.

A person charged in any State with treason, felony, or other crime, who shall flee from justice, and be found in another State, shall, on demand of the executive authority of the State from which he fled, be delivered up, to be removed to the State having jurisdiction of the crime.

No person held to service or labor in one State, under the laws thereof, escaping into another, shall, in consequence of any law or regulation therein, be discharged from such service or labor, but shall be delivered up on claim of the party to whom such service or labor may be due.

Sec. 3. New States may be admitted by the Congress into this Union ; but no new State shall be formed or erected within the jurisdiction of any other State ; nor any State be formed by the junction of two or more States, or parts of States, without the consent of the legislatures of the States concerned as well as of the Congress.

The Congress shall have power to dispose of and make all needful rules and regulations respecting the territory or other property belonging to the United States ; and nothing in this Constitution shall be so construed as to prejudice any claims of the United States, or of any particular State.

Sec. 4. The United States shall guarantee to every State in this Union a republican form of government, and shall protect each of them against invasion ; and on application of the legislature, or of the executive (when the legislature cannot be convened), against domestic violence.

ARTICLE V.

The Congress, whenever two thirds of both Houses shall deem it necessary, shall propose amendments to this Constitution, or, on the application of the legislatures of two thirds of the several States, shall call a convention for proposing amendments, which, in either case, shall be valid to all intents and purposes, as part of this Constitution, when ratified by the legislatures of three fourths of the several States, or by conventions in three fourths thereof, as the one or the other mode of ratification may be proposed by the Congress; provided that no amendments which may be made prior to the year one thousand eight hundred and eight shall in any manner affect the first and fourth clauses in the ninth section of the first article; and that no State, without its consent, shall be deprived of its equal suffrage in the Senate.

ARTICLE VI.

All debts contracted and engagements entered into, before the adoption of this

Constitution, shall be as valid against the United States under this Constitution, as under the Confederation.

This Constitution, and the laws of the United States which shall be made in pursuance thereof; and all treaties made, or which shall be made, under the authority of the United States, shall be the supreme law of the land; and the judges in every State shall be bound thereby, any thing in the constitution or laws of any State to the contrary notwithstanding.

The Senators and Representatives before mentioned, and the members of the several State legislatures, and all the executive and judicial officers, both of the United States and of the several States, shall be bound, by oath or affirmation, to support this Constitution; but no religious test shall ever be required as a qualification to any office or public trust under the United States.

ARTICLE VII.

The ratification of the conventions of nine States shall be sufficient for the establishment of this Constitution between the States so ratifying the same.*

———

ARTICLES IN ADDITION TO, AND AMEND-
MENT OF, THE CONSTITUTION OF THE
UNITED STATES OF AMERICA, PRO-
POSED BY CONGRESS, AND RATIFIED BY
THE LEGISLATURES OF THE SEVERAL
STATES PURSUANT TO THE FIFTH AR-
TICLE OF THE ORIGINAL CONSTITU-
TION.†

ARTICLE I.

Congress shall make no law respecting an establishment of religion, or prohibiting the free exercise thereof ; or abridging the freedom of speech, or of the press ; or

* The text and punctuation of the Constitution, as above, conform to the document in the custody of the State Department.

† The first ten amendments to the Constitution were proposed to the legislatures of the several States by the First Congress on the 25th of September, 1789, and were ratified by the States between that date and December 15, 1791. There is no evidence on the journals of Congress that the legislatures of Connecticut, Georgia, and Massachusetts ratified them.

the right of the people peaceably to assemble, and to petition the Government for a redress of grievances.

ARTICLE II.

A well regulated militia, being necessary to the security of a free state, the right of the people to keep and bear arms shall not be infringed.

ARTICLE III.

No soldier shall, in time of peace, be quartered in any house, without the consent of the owner, nor in the time of war, but in a manner to be prescribed by law.

ARTICLE IV.

The right of the people to be secure in their persons, houses, papers, and effects, against unreasonable searches and seizures, shall not be violated, and no warrants shall issue, but upon probable cause, supported by oath or affirmation, and particularly describing the place to be searched, and the person or things to be seized.

ARTICLE V.

No person shall be held to answer for a capital, or otherwise infamous, crime, unless on a presentment or indictment of a grand jury, except in cases arising in the land or naval forces, or in the militia, when in actual service in time of war or public danger ; nor shall any person be subject for the same offence to be twice put in jeopardy of life or limb ; nor shall be compelled in any criminal case to be a witness against himself, nor be deprived of life, liberty, or property, without due process of law ; nor shall private property be taken for public use without just compensation.

ARTICLE VI.

In all criminal prosecutions the accused shall enjoy the right to a speedy and public trial, by an impartial jury of the State and district wherein the crime shall have been committed, which district shall have been previously ascertained by law, and to be informed of the nature and cause of the accusation ; to be confronted with the witnesses against him ; to have compulsory process for obtaining witnesses in his favor, and to have the assistance of counsel for his defence.

ARTICLE VII.

In suits at common law, where the value in controversy shall exceed twenty dollars, the right of trial by jury shall be preserved, and no fact tried by a jury shall be otherwise reëxamined in any court of the United States, than according to the rules of the common law.

ARTICLE VIII.

Excessive bail should not be required, nor excessive fines imposed, nor cruel and unusual punishments inflicted.

ARTICLE IX.

The enumeration in the Constitution, of certain rights, shall not be construed to deny or disparage others retained by the people.

ARTICLE X.

The powers not delegated to the United States by the Constitution, nor prohibited by it to the States, are reserved to the States respectively, or to the people.

ARTICLE XI.

The judicial power of the United States shall not be construed to extend to any suit in law or equity, commenced or prosecuted against one of the United States by citizens of another State, or by citizens or subjects of any foreign state.*

ARTICLE XII.

The electors shall meet in their respective States, and vote by ballot for President and Vice-President, one of whom, at least, shall not be an inhabitant

* The Eleventh Amendment was proposed to the legislatures of the several States by the Third Congress, on the 5th of September, 1794, and was declared, in a message from the President to Congress, dated the 8th of January, 1798, to have been ratified by the legislatures of three fourths of the States.

of the same State with themselves; they shall name in their ballots the person voted for as President, and in distinct ballots the person voted for as Vice-President, and they shall make distinct lists of all persons voted for as President, and of all persons voted for as Vice-President, and of the number of votes for each, which lists they shall sign and certify, and transmit sealed to the seat of the Government of the United States, directed to the President of the Senate. The President of the Senate shall, in the presence of the Senate and House of Representatives, open all the certificates and the votes shall then be counted. The person having the greatest number of votes for President, shall be the President, if such number be a majority of the whole number of electors appointed; and if no person have such majority, then from the persons having the highest numbers not exceeding three on the list of those voted for as President, the House of Representatives shall choose immediately, by ballot, the President. But in choosing the President, the votes shall be taken by States, the representation from each State having one vote ; a quorum for this purpose shall consist of a member or members from two thirds of the States, and a majority of all the States shall be necessary to a choice. And if the House of Representatives shall not choose a President, whenever the right of choice shall devolve upon them, before the fourth day of March next following, then the Vice-President shall act as President, as in the case of the death or other constitutional disability of the President.

The person having the greatest number of votes as Vice-President, shall be the Vice-President, if such number be a majority of the whole number of electors appointed, and if no person have a majority, then from the two highest numbers on the list, the Senate shall choose the Vice-President ; a quorum for the purpose shall consist of two thirds of the whole number of Senators, and a majority of the whole number shall be necessary to a choice. But no person constitutionally ineligible to the office of President shall be eligible to that of Vice-President of the United States.*

ARTICLE XIII.

Section 1. Neither slavery nor involuntary servitude, except as a punishment for crime whereof the party shall have been duly convicted, shall exist within the United States, or any place subject to their jurisdiction.

Sec. 2. Congress shall have power to enforce this article by appropriate legislation.†

*The Twelfth Amendment was proposed to the legislatures of the several States by the Eighth Congress, on the 12th of December, 1803, in lieu of the original third paragraph of Section 1. of Article II., and was declared in a proclamation of the Secretary of State, dated the 25th of September, 1804, to have been ratified by the legislatures of three fourths of the States.

† The Thirteenth Amendment was proposed to the legislatures of the several States by the Thirty-eighth Congress, on the 1st of February,

ARTICLE XIV.

Section 1. All persons born or naturalized in the United States, and subject to the jurisdiction thereof, are citizens of the United States and of the State wherein they reside. No State shall make or enforce any law which shall abridge the privileges or immunities of citizens of the United States ; nor shall any State deprive any person of life, liberty, or property, without due process of law ; nor deny to any person within its jurisdiction the equal protection of the laws.

Sec. 2. Representatives shall be apportioned among the several States according to their respective numbers,

1865, and was declared, in a proclamation of the Secretary of State, dated the 18th of December, 1865, to have been ratified by the legislatures of twenty-seven of the thirty-six States, viz.: Illinois, Rhode Island, Michigan, Maryland, New York, West Virginia, Maine, Kansas, Massachusetts, Pennsylvania, Virginia, Ohio, Missouri, Nevada, Indiana, Louisiana, Minnesota, Wisconsin, Vermont, Tennessee, Arkansas, Connecticut, New Hampshire, South Carolina, Alabama, North Carolina, and Georgia.

counting the whole number of persons in each State, excluding Indians not taxed. But when the right to vote at any election for the choice of electors for President and Vice-President of the United States, Representatives in Congress, the executive and judicial officers of the State, or the members of the legislature thereof, is denied to any of the male inhabitants of such State, being twenty-one years of age, and citizens of the United States, or in any way abridged, except for participation in rebellion, or other crime, the basis of representation therein shall be reduced in the proportion which the number of such male citizens shall bear to the whole number of male citizens twenty-one years of age in such State.

Sec. 3. No person shall be a Senator or Representative in Congress, or elector of President and Vice-President, or hold any office, civil or military, under the United States, or under any State, who, having previously taken an oath, as a member of Congress, or as an officer of the United States, or as a member of any State legislature, or as an executive or judicial officer of any State, to support the Constitution of the United States, shall have engaged in insurrection or rebellion against the same, or given aid or comfort to the enemies thereof. But Congress may, by a vote of two thirds of each House, remove such disability.

Sec. 4. The validity of the public debt of the United States, authorized by law, including debts incurred for payment of pensions and bounties for services in suppressing insurrection or rebellion, shall not be questioned. But neither the United States nor any State shall assume or pay any debt or obligation incurred in aid of insurrection or rebellion against the United States, or any claim for the loss or emancipation of any slave ; but all such debts, obligations, and claims shall be held illegal and void.

Sec. 5. The Congress shall have power

to enforce, by appropriate legislation, the provisions of this article.*

ARTICLE XV.

Section 1. The right of citizens of the United States to vote shall not be denied or abridged by the United States or any State on account of race, color, or previous condition of servitude.

Sec. 2. The Congress shall have power to enforce this article by appropriate legislation.†

* The Fourteenth Amendment was proposed to the legislatures of the several States by the Thirty-ninth Congress, on the 16th of June, 1866. On the 28th of July, 1868, the Secretary of State issued a proclamation declaring that this amendment had been ratified by the legislatures of thirty of the thirty-six States.

† The Fifteenth Amendment was proposed to the legislatures of the several States by the Fortieth Congress, on the 27th of February, 1869, and was declared, in a proclamation of the Secretary of State, dated March 30, 1870, to have been ratified by the legislatures of twenty-nine of the thirty-seven States.

WASHINGTON'S CIRCULAR LETTER OF CONGRATULATION AND ADVICE TO THE GOVERNORS OF THE THIRTEEN STATES

WASHINGTON'S CIRCULAR LETTER OF CONGRATULATION AND ADVICE TO THE GOVERNORS OF THE THIRTEEN STATES.*

* See Appendix, page 189.

HEAD-QUARTERS, NEWBURG, June 18, 1783.

SIR :—The great object for which I had the honor to hold an appointment in the service of my country being accomplished, I am now preparing to resign it into the hands of Congress, and return to that domestic retirement which, it is well known, I left with the greatest reluctance ; a retirement for which I have never ceased to sigh through a long and painful absence, in which (remote from the noise and trouble of the world) I meditate to pass the remainder of life in a state of undisturbed repose ; but, before I carry this resolution into effect, I think it a duty incumbent on me to make this, my last, official communication, to congratulate you on the glorious events which heaven has been pleased to produce in our favor, to offer my sentiments respecting some important subjects, which appear to me to be intimately connected with the tranquillity of the United States, to take my leave of your Excellency as a public character, and to give my final blessing to that country in whose service I have spent the prime of my life; for whose sake I have consumed so many anxious days and watchful nights; and whose happiness, being extremely dear to me, will always constitute no inconsiderable part of my own.

Impressed with the liveliest sensibility on this pleasing occasion, I will claim the indulgence of dilating the more copiously on the subject of our mutual felicitation. When we consider the magnitude of the prize we contended for, the doubtful nature of the contest, and the favorable manner in which it has terminated, we

shall find the greatest possible reason
for gratitude and rejoicing ; this is a theme
that will afford infinite delight to every
benevolent and liberal mind, whether the
event in contemplation be considered as
a source of present enjoyment or the parent of future happiness ; and we shall
have equal occasion to felicitate ourselves
on the lot which Providence has assigned
us, whether we view it in a natural, a
political, or moral point of view.

The citizens of America, placed in the
most enviable condition, as the sole lords
and proprietors of a vast tract of continent,
comprehending all the various soils and
climates of the world, and abounding
with all the necessaries and conveniences
of life, are now, by the late satisfactory
pacification, acknowledged to be possessed
of absolute freedom and independency ;
they are, from this period, to be considered as the actors on a most conspicuous
theatre, which seems to be peculiarly de-
signed by Providence for the display of
human greatness and felicity ; here they

are not only surrounded with every thing
that can contribute to the completion of
private and domestic enjoyment, but
heaven has crowned all its other blessings by giving a surer opportunity for
political happiness than any other nation
has ever been favored with. Nothing can
illustrate these observations more forcibly
than the recollection of the happy con-
juncture of times and circumstances under which our republic assumed its rank
among the nations. The foundation of
our empire was not laid in a gloomy age
of ignorance and superstition, but at an
epoch when the rights of mankind were
better understood and more clearly defined
than at any former period ; researches of
the human mind after social happiness
have been carried to a great extent ; the
treasures of knowledge acquired by the
labors of philosophers, sages, and legisla-
tors, through a long succession of years,
are laid open for us, and their collected
wisdom may be happily applied in the
establishment of our forms of govern-

ment ; the free cultivation of letters, the unbounded extension of commerce, the progressive refinement of manners, the growing liberality of sentiment, and, above all, the pure and benign light of revelation, have had a meliorating influence on mankind, and increased the blessings of society. At this auspicious period the United States came into existence as a nation, and if their citizens should not be completely free and happy, the fault will be entirely their own.

Such is our situation, and such are our prospects; but notwithstanding the cup of blessing is thus reached out to us —notwithstanding happiness is ours, if we have a disposition to seize the occasion, and make it our own ; yet, it appears to me, there is an option still left to the United States of America, whether they will be respectable and prosperous or contemptible and miserable as a nation. This is the time of their political probation ; this is the moment when the eyes of the world are turned upon them ; this is the time to establish or ruin their national character forever; this is the favorable time to give such a tone to the federal government as will enable it to answer the ends of its institution; or this may be the ill-fated moment for relaxing the powers of the nation, annihilating the cement of the confederation, and exposing us to become the sport of European politics, which may play one state against another to prevent their growing importance, and to serve their own interested purposes. For, according to the system of policy the states shall adopt at this moment, they will stand or fall; and, by their confirmation or lapse, it is yet to be decided whether the revolution must ultimately be considered as a blessing or a curse; a blessing or a curse not to the present age alone, for with our fate will the destiny of unborn millions be involved.

With this conviction of the importance of the present crisis, silence in me would be a crime. I will therefore

speak to your Excellency the language
of freedom and sincerity, without dis-
guise. I am aware, however, those who
differ from me in political sentiments
may perhaps remark, I am stepping out
of the proper line of my duty ; and they
may possibly ascribe to arrogance or ostentation what I know is alone the result
of the purest intention ; but the rectitude
of my own heart, which disdains such
unworthy motives—the part I have hitherto acted in life—the determination I
have formed of not taking any share in
public business hereafter—the ardent desire I feel and shall continue to mani-
fest, of quietly enjoying in private life,
after all the toils of war, the benefits of
a wise and liberal government—will, I
flatter myself, sooner or later, convince
my countrymen that I could have no
sinister views in delivering, with so little
reserve, the opinions contained in this
Address.

There are four things which I humbly
conceive are essential to the well-being,

I may even venture to say, to the existence of the United States, as an independent power :

1st.—An indissoluble union of the states under one federal head.

2ndly.—A sacred regard to public justice.

3rdly.—The adoption of a proper peace establishment, And.

4thly.—The prevalence of that pacific and friendly disposition among the people of the United States, which will induce them to forget their local prejudices and policies, to make those mutual concessions which are requisite to the general prosperity, and, in some instances, to sacrifice their individual advantages to the interest of the community.

These are the pillars on which the glorious fabric of our independency and national character must be supported. Liberty is the basis, and whoever would dare to sap the foundation, or overturn the structure, under whatever specious pretext he may attempt it, will merit the bitterest execration and the severest punishment which can be inflicted by his injured country.

On the three first articles I will make a few observations, leaving the last to the good sense and serious consideration of those immediately concerned.

Under the first head, although it may not be necessary or proper for me in this place to enter into a particular disquisition of the principals of the union, and to take up the great question which has been frequently agitated, whether it be expedient and requisite for the states to delegate a large proportion of power to Congress, or not ; yet it will be a part of my duty, and that of every true patriot, to assert, without reserve, and to insist upon the following positions. That unless the states will suffer Congress to exercise those prerogatives they are undoubtedly invested with by the constitution, every thing must very rapidly tend to anarchy and confusion.—That it is indispensable to the happiness of the individual states, that there should be lodged, somewhere, a supreme power, to regulate and govern the general concerns of the confederated republic, without which the union cannot be of long duration.—That there must be a faithful and pointed compliance on the part of every state with the late proposals and demands of Congress, or the most fatal consequences will ensue. That whatever measures have a tendency to dissolve the union, or contribute to violate or lessen sovereign authority, ought to be considered as hostile to the liberty and independency of America, and the authors of them treated accordingly.—And lastly, that unless we can be enabled by the concurrence of the states, to participate of the fruits of the revolution, and enjoy the essential benefits of civil society, under a form of government so free and uncorrupted, so happily guarded against the danger of oppression, as has been devised and adopted by the articles of confederation, it will be a subject of regret, that so much blood and treasure have been lavished for no purpose; that so many sufferings have been encountered without a compensation, and so many sacrifices have been made in vain. Many other considerations might here be adduced to prove, that without an entire conformity to the spirit of the union, we cannot exist as an independent power. It will be sufficient for my purpose to mention but one or two, which seem to me of the greatest importance. It is only in our united character, as an empire, that our independence is acknowledged, that our power can be regarded, or our credit supported among foreign nations. The treaties of the European powers with the United States of America, will have no validity on the dissolution of the union. We shall be left nearly in a state of nature; or we may find, by our own unhappy experience, that there is a natural and necessary progression from the extreme of anarchy to the extreme of tyrany; and that arbitrary power is most easily established on the ruins of liberty abused to licentiousness.

As to the second article, which respects the performance of public justice, Congress have, in their late Address to the United States, almost exhausted the subject ; they have explained their ideas so fully, and have enforced the obligations the states are under to render complete justice to all the public creditors, with so much dignity and energy that, in my opinion, no real friend to the honour and independency of America can hesitate a single moment respecting the propriety of complying with the just and honourable measures proposed. If their arguments do not produce conviction, I know of nothing that will have greater influence, especially when we reflect that the system referred to, being the result of the collected wisdom of the continent, must be esteemed, if not perfect, certainly the least objectionable of any that could be devised ; and that if it should not be carried into immediate execution, a national bankruptcy, with all its deplorable consequences, will take place before any different plan can possibly be proposed or adopted; so pressing are the present circumstances, and such is the alternative now offered to the states.

The ability of the country to discharge the debts which have been incurred in its defence is not to be doubted. An inclination, I flatter myself, will not be wanting; the path of our duty is plain before us; honesty will be found, on every experiment, to be the best and only true policy. Let us then, as a nation, be just; let us fulfil the public contracts which Congress had undoubtedly a right to make for the purpose of carrying on the war, with the same good faith we suppose ourselves bound to perform our private engagements. In the meantime let our attention to the cheerful performance of their proper business, as individuals, and as members of society, be earnestly inculcated on the citizens of America; then will they strengthen the bands of government, and be happy under its protection. Every one will reap the fruit of his labours; every one will enjoy his own acquisitions, without molestation and without danger.

In this state of absolute freedom and perfect security, who will grudge to yield a very little of his property to support the common interests of society, and ensure the protection of government? Who does not remember the frequent declarations at the commencement of the war, that we should be completely satisfied if at the expense of one half, we could defend the remainder of our possessions? Where is the man to be found, who wishes to remain indebted for the defence of his own person and property at the exertions, the bravery, and the blood of others, without making one generous effort to pay the debt of honour and of gratitude? In what part of the continent shall we find any man, or body of men, who would not blush to stand up and propose measures purposely calculated to rob the soldier

of his stipend, and the public creditor of
his due? And were it possible that such
a flagrant instance of injustice could ever
happen, would it not excite the general
indignation and tend to bring down upon
the authors of such measures, the ag-
gravated vengeance of heaven? If, after
all, a spirit of disunion, or a temper of
obstinacy and perverseness should mani-
fest itself in any of the states; if such
an ungracious disposition should attempt
to frustrate all the happy effects that
might be expected to flow from the
Union; if there should be a refusal to
comply with the requisitions for funds to
discharge the annual interest of the public
debts, and if that refusal should revive all
those jealousies, and produce all those
evils which are now happily removed—
Congress, who have in all their transactions shewn a great degree of magnanimity and justice, will stand justified in the
sight of God and man! And that State
alone, which puts itself in opposition to
the aggregate wisdom of the continent,

and follows such mistaken and pernicious councils, will be responsible for all the consequences.

For my own part, conscious of having acted, while a servant of the public, in the manner I conceived best suited to promote the real interests of my country; having, in consequence of my fixed belief, in some measure, pledged myself to the army, that their country would finally do them complete and ample justice, and not willing to conceal any instance of my official conduct from the eyes of the world, I have thought proper to transmit to your excellency the inclosed collection of papers, relative to the half-pay and commutation granted by Congress to the officers of the army: from these communications, my decided sentiment will be clearly comprehended, together with the conclusive reasons, which induced me at an early period, to reccommend the adoption of this measure in the most earnest and serious manner. As the proceedings of Congress, the army, and myself, are open to all, and contain, in my opinion, sufficient information to remove the prejudice and errors which may have been entertained by any, I think it unnecessary to say any thing more, than just to observe, that the resolutions of Congress, now alluded to, are undoubtedly and absolutely binding upon the United States as the most solemn acts of confederation or legislation.

As to the idea, which I am informed, has in some instances prevailed, that the half-pay and commutation are to be regarded merely in the odious light of a pension, it ought to be exploded forever : that provision should be reviewed, as it really was, a reasonable compensation offered by Congress, at a time when they had nothing else to give to officers of the army, for services then to be performed : it was the only means to prevent a total deriliction of the service ; it was part of their hire. I may be allowed to say, it was the price of their blood, and of your independency ; it is therefore more than a common debt, it is a debt of honour ; it can never be considered as a pension or gratuity, nor cancelled until it is fairly discharged.

With regard to the distinction between officers and soldiers, it is sufficient that the uniform experience of every nation of the world combined with our own proves the utility and propriety of the discrimination. Rewards, in proportion to the aid the public draws from them, are unquestionably due to all its servants. In some lines, the soldiers have perhaps generally had as ample compensation for their services, by the large bounties which have been paid to them, as their officers will receive in the proposed commutation ; in others, if besides the donation of land, the payment of arrearages of cloathing and wages (in which article all the component parts of the army must be put upon the same footing) we take into the estimate, the bounties many of the soldiers have received, and the gratuity of one year's full pay, which is promised to all, possibly their situation (every circumstance being duly considered) will not be deemed less legible than that of the officers. Should a farther reward, however, be judged equitable, I will venture to assert, no man will enjoy greater satisfaction than myself, in an exemption from taxes for a limited time (which has been petitioned for in some instances) or any other adequate immunity or compensation granted to the brave defenders of their countrie's cause : but neither the adoption or rejection of this proposition will, in any manner affect, much less militate against the act of Congress, by which they have offered five years full pay, in lieu of the half pay for life, which had been before promised to the officers of the army.

Before I conclude the subject on public justice, I cannot omit to mention the obligations this country is under to that meritorious class of veterans, the non-commissioned officers and privates, who have been discharged for inability, in consequence of the resolution of Congress, of the 23d of April, 1782, on an annual pension for life. Their peculiar sufferings, their singular merits and claims to that provision need only to be known, to interest the feelings of humanity in their behalf. Nothing but a punctual payment of their annual allowance can rescue them from the most complicated misery; and nothing could be a more melancholy sight, than to behold those who have shed their blood, or lost their limbs in the service of their country, without a shelter, without a friend, and without the means of obtaining any of the comforts or necessaries of life, compelled to beg their daily bread from door to door. Suffer me to recommend those of this description, belonging to your state, to the warmest patronage of your excellency and your legislature.

It is necessary to say but a few words on the third topic which was proposed, and which regards particularly the defence of the republic. As there can be little doubt but Congress will recommend a proper peace establishment for the United States, in which a due attention will be paid to the importance of placing the militia of the union upon a regular and respectable footing; if this should be the case, I should beg leave to urge the great advantage of it in the strongest terms.

The militia of this country must be considered as the palladium of our security, and the first effectual resort in case of hostility; it is essential, therefore, that the same system should pervade the whole, that the formation and discipline of the militia of the continent should be absolutely uniform; and the same species of arms, accoutrements, and military apparatus, should be introduced in every part of the United States. No one, who has not learned it from experience, can conceive the difficulty, expense, and confusion which result from a contrary system, or the vague arrangements which have hitherto prevailed.

If, in treating of political points, a greater latitude than usual has been taken in the course of this Address, the importance of the crisis, and the magnitude of the objects in discussion, must be my apology ; it is, however, neither my wish nor expectation, that the preceding observations should claim any regard, except so far as they shall appear to be dictated by a good intention ; consonant to the immutable rules of justice ; calculated to produce a liberal system of policy, and founded on whatever experience may have been acquired by a long and close attention to public business. Here I might speak with more confidence, from my actual observations ; and if it would not swell this letter (already too prolix) beyond the bounds I had prescribed myself, I could demonstrate to every mind, open to conviction, that in less time, and with much less expense than had been incurred, the war might have brought to the same happy conclusion, if the resources of the continent could have been properly called forth ; that the distresses and disappointments which have very often occurred, have, in too many instances, resulted more from a want of energy in the continental government, than a deficiency of means in the particular States : that the inefficacy of the measures, arising from the want of an adequate authority in the supreme power, from a partial compliance with the requisitions of Congress in some of the states, and from a failure of punctuality in others, while they tended to damp the zeal of those who were more willing to exert themselves, served also to accumulate the expenses of war, and to frustrate the best concerted plans ; and that the discouragement occasioned by the complicated difficulties and embarrassments, in which our affairs were by this means involved, would have long ago produced the dissolution of any army, less patient, less virtuous, and less persevering than that which I have had the honour to command. But while I mention those things, which are notorious facts, as the defects of our federal constitution, particularly in the prosecution of a war, I beg it may be understood, that as I have ever taken a pleasure in gratefully acknowledging the assistance and support I have derived from every class of citizens; so shall I always be happy to do justice to the unparalleled exertions of the individual states, on many interesting occasions.

I have thus freely disclosed what I wished to make known before I surrendered up my public trust to those who committed it to me : the task is now accomplished. I now bid adieu to your excellency, as the chief magistrate of your state; at the same time I bid a last farewell to the cares of office, and all the employments of public life.

It remains, then, to be my final and only request, that your excellency will communicate these sentiments to your legislature, at their next meeting, and that they may be considered as the legacy of one who has ardently wished, on all occasions, to be useful to his country, and who, even in the shade of retirement, will not fail to implore the divine benediction upon it.

I now make it my earnest prayer, that God would have you, and the state over which you preside, in his holy protection ; that He would incline the hearts of the citizens to cultivate a spirit of subordination and obedience to the government ; to entertain a brotherly affection and love for one another, for their fellow-citizens of the United States at large ; and particularly for their bretheren who have served in the field ; and finally, that He would most graciously be pleased to dispose us all to do justice, to love mercy, and to demean ourselves with that charity, humility, and pacific temper of the mind, which were the characteristics of the divine author of our blessed religion ;

without an humble imitation of whose example, in these things, we can never hope to be a happy nation.

I have the honour to be, with much esteem and respect, sir, your excellency's most obedient, and most humble servant,

G. WASHINGTON.

WASHINGTON'S INAUGURAL ADDRESS

G. Washington

INAUGURAL ADDRESS.*

FELLOW-CITIZENS of the Senate, and of the House of Representatives.—Among the vicissitudes incident to life, no event could have filled me with greater anxieties, than that of which the notification was transmitted by your order, and received on the fourteenth day of the present month. On the one hand, I was summoned by my country, whose voice I can never hear but with veneration and love, from a retreat which I had chosen with the fondest predilection, and in my flattering hopes with an immutable

* See Appendix, page 195.

decision as the asylum of my declining years ;* a retreat which was rendered every day more necessary, as well as more dear to me, by the addition of habit to inclination, and of frequent interruptions in my health to the gradual waste committed on it by time. On the other hand, the magnitude and difficulty of the trust, to which the voice of my country called me, being sufficient to waken in the wisest and most experienced of her citizens a distrustful scrutiny into his own qualifications, could not but overwhelm with despondence one, who, inheriting inferior endowments from nature, and unpractised in the duties of civil administration, ought to be peculiarly conscious of his own deficiencies. In this conflict of emotions, all I dare aver is, that it has been my faithful study to collect my duty from a just appreciation of every circumstance by which it might be affected. All I dare hope is, that if, in executing this task, I have been too much swayed by a grateful remembrance of former in-

* See Appendix, page 105.

stances, or by an affectionate sensibility to this transcendent proof of the confidence of my fellow-citizens, and have thence too little consulted my incapacity as well as disinclination for the weighty and untried cares before me, my error will be palliated by the motives which misled me, and its consequences be judged by my country with some share of the partiality in which they originated.

Such being the impression under which I have, in obedience to the public summons, repaired to the present station, it would be peculiarly improper to omit, in this first official act, my fervent supplications to that Almighty Being who rules over the universe—who presides in the councils of nations—and whose providential aids can supply every human defect, that His benediction may consecrate to the liberties and happiness of the people of the United States, a government instituted by themselves for these essential purposes ; and may enable every instrument, employed in its administration, to execute with success the functions allotted to his charge. In tendering this homage to the great Author of every public and private good, I assure myself that it expresses your sentiments not less than my own, nor those of my fellow-citizens at large, less than either. No people can be bound to acknowledge and adore the invisible hand which conducts the affairs of men, more than the people of the United States. Every step by which they have advanced to the character of an independent nation, seems to have been distinguished by some token of providential agency ; and in the important revolution just accomplished in the system of their united government, the tranquil deliberations and voluntary consent of so many distinct communities, from which the event has resulted, cannot be compared with the means by which most governments have been established, without some return of pious gratitude, along with an humble anticipation of the future blessings which the past seems to presage.

These reflections, arising out of the present crisis, have forced themselves too strongly on my mind to be suppressed. You will join with me, I trust, in thinking that there are none under the influence of which the proceedings of a new and free government can more auspiciously commence.

By the article establishing the executive department, it is made the duty of the President "to recommend to your consideration such measures as he shall judge necessary and expedient." The circumstances under which I now meet you will acquit me from entering into that subject, further than to refer to the great constitutional charter under which you are assembled; and which, in defining your powers, designates the objects to which your attention is to be given. It will be more consistent with those circumstances, and far more congenial with the feelings which actuate me, to substitute in place of a recommendation of particular measures the tribute that is due to

the talents, the rectitude, and the patriotism which adorn the characters selected to devise and adopt them. In these
honorable qualifications, I behold the
surest pledges, that as, on one side, no
local prejudices or attachments, no separate views, nor party animosities, will mis-
direct the comprehensive and equal eye
which ought to watch over this great
assemblage of communities and interests ;
so on another, that the foundations of
our national policy will be laid in the
pure and immutable principles of private
morality ; and the pre-eminence of free
government be exemplified by all the
attributes which can win the affections of
its citizens, and command the respect of
the world. . I dwell on this prospect with
every satisfaction which an ardent love
for my country can inspire ; since there
is no truth more thoroughly established
than that there exists in the economy and
course of nature an indissoluble union
between virtue and happiness, between
duty and advantage, between the genuine

maxims of an honest and magnanimous policy and the solid rewards of public prosperity and felicity ; since we ought to be no less persuaded that the propitious smiles of Heaven can never be expected on a nation that disregards the eternal rules of order and right which Heaven itself has ordained ; and since the preservation of the sacred fire of liberty and the destiny of the republican model of government are justly considered as deeply, perhaps as finally, staked on the experiment entrusted to the hands of the American people.

Besides the ordinary objects submitted to your care, it will remain with your judgment to decide how far an exercise of the occasional power delegated by the Fifth Article of the Constitution is rendered expedient at the present juncture by the nature of objections which have been urged against the system, or by the degree of inquietude which has given birth to them. Instead of undertaking particular recommendations on this subject, in

which I could be guided by no lights derived from official opportunities, I shall
again give way to my entire confidence
in your discernment and pursuit of the
public good ; for I assure myself that
whilst you carefully avoid every altera-
tion which might endanger the benefits
of an united and effective government, or
which ought to await the future lessons
of experience, a reverence for the charac-
teristic rights of freemen and a regard
for the public harmony will sufficiently
influence your deliberations on the question how far the former may be more im-
pregnably fortified, or the latter be safely
and advantageously promoted.

To the preceding observations I have
one to add, which will be most properly
addressed to the House of Representatives.
It concerns myself, and will therefore be
as brief as possible. When I was first
honored with a call into the service of my
country, then on the eve of an arduous
struggle for its liberties, the light in
which I contemplated my duty required

that I should renounce every pecuniary compensatiom. From this resolution I have in no instance departed. And being still under the impressions which produced it I must decline, as inapplicable to myself, any share in the personal emoluments which may be indispensably included in a permanent provision for the executive department ; and must accordingly pray that the pecuniary estimates for the station in which I am placed may, during my continuance in it, be limited to such actual expenditures as the public good may be thought to require.

Having thus imparted to you my sentiments, as they have been awakened by the occasion which brings us together, I shall take my present leave ; but not without resorting once more to the benign Parent of the human race, in humble supplication, that since He has been pleased to favor the American people with opportunities for deliberating in perfect tranquillity, and dispositions for deciding with unparalleled unanimity on a form of government for the security of their union and the advancement of their happiness; so His divine blessings may be equally conspicuous in the enlarged views, the temperate consultations, and the wise measures on which the success of this government must depend.

WASHINGTON'S SECOND INAUG-
URAL ADDRESS

SECOND INAUGURAL ADDRESS.*

PHILADELPHIA, MARCH 4, 1793.

FELLOW-CITIZENS. — I am again called upon by the voice of my country to execute the functions of its Chief Magistrate. When the occasion proper for it shall arrive, I shall endeavor to express the high sense I entertain of this distinguished honor, and of the confidence which has been reposed in me by the people of the United States of America. Previous to the execution of any official act of the President, the Constitution requires an oath of office. This oath I am now about to take and in your presence; that if it shall be found, during my ad-

* See Appendix, page 196.

ministration of the government, I have, in any instance, violated, willingly or knowingly, the injunction therof, I may (besides incurring constitutional punishment) be subject to the upbraidings of all who are now witnesses of the present solemn ceremony.

WASHINGTON'S FAREWELL
ADDRESS

FAREWELL ADDRESS.*

[The original MS. of the Farewell Address, in Washington's handwriting, and with his revisions and alterations, having been purchased by James Lenox, Esquire, of New York, that gentleman caused a few copies of it, with some illustrative documents, to be printed for private distribution. By permission of Mr. Lenox it is here reprinted, with the alterations, and with his explanatory remarks.]

PREFACE.†

THIS reprint of Washington's Farewell Address to the people of the United States is made from the original manuscript recently sold in Philadelphia by the administrators of the late Mr. David C. Claypoole, in whose possession it had been from the date of its first publication. The paper is *entirely* in the autograph of Washington ; no one acquainted with his handwriting can inspect it, and doubt for a moment the statements to that effect made by Mr. Claypoole and Mr. Rawle.

Upon examining the manuscript, it was found that, in addition to its importance as an historical document, and its value from being in the autograph of Washington, it was of great interest as a literary curiosity, and threw light upon the disputed question of the authorship of the Address. It clearly shows the process by which that paper was wrought into the form in which it was first given to the public; and notes written on the margin of passages and paragraphs, which have been erased, prove, almost beyond a doubt, that this draft was submitted to the judgment of other persons. Such memoranda were unnecessary, either for Washington's own direction on a subsequent revision, or for the guidance of the printer; but he might very naturally thus note the reasons which had led him to make the alterations before he asked the advice and opinion of his friends. It seems probable, therefore, that this is the very draft sent to General Hamilton and Chief-Justice Jay, as related in the letter of the latter. Some of the alterations, however, were evidently made during the writing of the paper; for in a few instances a part, and even the whole, of a sentence is struck out, which afterwards occurs in the body of the address.

Mr. Claypoole's description of the appearance of the manuscript is very accurate. There are many alterations, corrections, and interlineations ; and whole sentences and paragraphs are sometimes obliterated. All these, however, have been deciphered without much trouble, and carefully noted.

It was thought best to leave the text in this edition as it was first printed ; only two slight verbal variations were found between the corrected manuscript and the common printed copies. All the interlineations and alterations are inserted in brackets [ ], and where, in any case, words or sentences have been struck out, either with or without corrections in the text to supply their place, these portions have been deciphered and are printed in notes at the foot of the page. The reader will thus be enabled to perceive at a glance the changes made in the composition of the Address ; and if the draft made by General Hamilton, and read by him to Mr. Jay, should be published, it will be seen how far Washington adopted the modifications and suggestions made by them.

When this preface was thus far prepared for the press, an opportunity was afforded, through the kindness of John C. Hamilton, Esquire, to examine several letters which passed between Washington and General Hamilton relating to

the Address, and also a copy of it in the handwriting of the latter. It appears from these
communications that the President, both in
sending to him a rough draft of the document,
and at subsequent dates, requested him to prepare such an Address as he thought would be
appropriate to the occasion ; that Washington
consulted him particularly, and most minutely,
on many points connected with it ; and that at
different times General Hamilton did forward to
the President three drafts of such a paper. The
first was sent back to him with suggestions for
its correction and enlargement ; from the second
draft thus altered and improved, the manuscript
now printed may be supposed to have been prepared by Washington, and transmitted for final
examination to General Hamilton and Judge
Jay ; and with it the third draft was returned to
the President, and may probably yet be found
among his papers.

The copy in the possession of Mr. Hamilton
is probably the second of these three drafts ; it
is very much altered and corrected throughout.
In comparing it with that in Washington's
autograph, the sentiments are found to be the
same, and the words used are very frequently
identical. Some of the passages erased in the
manuscript are in the draft ; three paragraphs,
namely, those on pages 50, 51, and 52, have

nothing corresponding to them in the draft ; but a space is left in it, evidently for the insertion of additional matter. The comparison of these two papers is exceedingly curious. It is difficult to conceive how two persons should express the same ideas in substantially the same language, and yet with much diversity in the construction of the sentences and the position of the words.

J. L.

NEW YORK, *April* 12, 1850.

FAREWELL ADDRESS.

FRIENDS, AND FELLOW-CITIZENS.—
The period for a new election of a Citizen, to administer the Executive Government of the United States, being not far distant, and the time actually arrived, when your thoughts must be employed in designating the person who is to be clothed with that important trust [*], it appears to me proper, especially as it may conduce to a more distinct expression of the public voice, that I should now apprise you of the resolution I have formed, to decline being considered among the number of those out of whom a choice is to be made.

* for another term

I beg you, at the same time, to do me the justice to be assured that this resolution has not been taken without a strict regard to all the considerations appertaining to the relation which binds a dutiful citizen to his country—and that, in withdrawing the tender of service which silence in my situation might imply, I am influenced by no diminution of zeal for your future interest, no deficiency of grateful respect for your past kindness; but [am supported by]* a full conviction that the step is compatible with both.

The acceptance of, and continuance hitherto in, the office to which your suffrages have twice called me, have been a uniform sacrifice of inclination to the opinion of duty, and to a deference for what appeared to be your desire. I constantly hoped that it would have been much earlier in my power, consistently with motives which I was not at liberty to disregard, to return to that retirement

* act under

from which I had been reluctantly drawn. The strength of my inclination to do this, previous to the last election, had even led to the preparation of an address to declare it to you; but mature reflection on the then perplexed and critical posture of our affairs with foreign Nations, and the unanimous advice of persons entitled to my confidence, impelled me to abandon the idea.

I rejoice that the state of your concerns, external as well as internal, no longer renders the pursuit of inclination incompatible with the sentiment of duty, or propriety; and [am persuaded] * whatever partiality [may be retained]† for my services, [that]‡ in the present circumstances of our country [you] will not disapprove my determination to retire.

The impressions, [with]‖ which I first [undertook] § the arduous trust, were explained on the proper occasion. In the

* that   † any portion of you may yet retain
‡ even they   ‖ under   § accepted

discharge of this trust, I will only say that I have, with good intentions, contributed [towards]* the organization and administration of the government, the best exertions of which a very fallible judgment was capable. Not unconscious, in the outset, of the inferiority of my qualifications, experience in my own eyes, [perhaps] still more in the eyes of others, has [strengthened]† the motives to diffidence of myself; and every day the increasing weight of years admonishes me more and more, that the shade of retirement is as necessary to me as it will be welcome. Satisfied that if any circumstances have given peculiar value to my services, they were temporary, I have the consolation to believe, that, while choice and prudence invite me to quit the political scene, patriotism does not forbid it. [‡]

* to   † not lessened
‡ May I also have that of knowing, in my retreat, that the involuntary errors, I have probably committed, have been the sources of no serious or lasting mischief to our country. I

In looking forward to the moment, which is [intended] to terminate the career of my public life, my feelings do not permit me to suspend the deep acknowledgment [of]* that debt of gratitude which I owe to my beloved country, —for the many honors it has conferred upon me; still more for the stedfast confidence with which it has supported me; and for the opportunities I have thence enjoyed of manifesting my inviolable attachment, by services faithful and persevering, though [in usefulness unequal]† to my zeal. If benefits have resulted to our country from these services, let it always be remembered to your praise,

may then expect to realize, without alloy, the sweet enjoyment of partaking, in the midst of my fellow-citizens, the benign influence of good laws under a free government; the ever favorite object of my heart, and the happy reward, I trust, of our mutual cares, dangers, and labours.

(In the margin opposite this paragraph is the following note in Washington's autograph also erased, " obliterated to avoid the imputation of affected modesty.")

* demanded by   † unequal in usefulness

and as an instructive example in our annals, that, [*] under circumstances in which the Passions agitated in every direction were liable to [mislead],† amidst appearances sometimes dubious, vicissitudes of fortune often discouraging—in situations in which not unfrequently want of success has countenanced the spirit of criticism [the constancy of your support] was the essential prop of the efforts and [a]‡ guarantee of the plans by which they were effected. Profoundly penetrated with this idea, I shall carry it with me to the grave, as a strong incitement to unceasing vows [||] that Heaven may continue to you the choicest tokens of its beneficence—that your union and brotherly affection may be perpetual—that the free constitution, which is the work of your hands, may be sacredly maintained—that its administration in

---

* the constancy of your support
† wander and fluctuate
‡ the
|| the only return I can henceforth make

every department may be stamped with wisdom and virtue—that, in fine, the happiness of the people of these States, under the auspices of liberty, may be made complete, by so careful a preservation and so prudent a use of this blessing as will acquire to them the glory [*] of recommending it to the applause, the affection, and adoption of every nation which is yet a stranger to it.

Here, perhaps, I ought to stop. But a solicitude for your welfare which cannot end but with my life, and the apprehension of danger, natural to that solicitude [urge me, on an occasion like the present, to offer] † to your solemn contemplation, and to recommend to your frequent review, some sentiments which are the result of much reflection, of no inconsiderable observation [‡], and which ap-

---

* or satisfaction
† encouraged by the remembrance of your indulgent reception of my sentiments on an occasion not dissimilar to the present, urge me to offer
‡ and experience

pear to me all important to the permanency of your felicity as a people. These
will be offered to you with the more freedom as you can only see in them, the
disinterested warnings of a departed
friend, who can [possibly] have no personal motive to bias his counsels. [Nor
can I forget, as an encouragement to it,
your indulgent reception of my sentiments on a former and not dissimilar
occasion.]

Interwoven as is the love of liberty
with every ligament of your hearts, no
recommendation of mine is necessary to
fortify or confirm the attachment.

The Unity of Government which con-
stitutes you one people, is also now dear
to you. It is justly so ;—for it is a main
Pillar in the Edifice of your real independence ; [the support] of your tranquillity at home ; your peace abroad ; of
your safety ; [*] of your prosperity [†] ; of
that very liberty which you so highly
prize. But, as it is easy to foresee, that

* in every relation   † in every shape

from [different]* causes, and from different quarters, much pains will be taken, many artifices employed, to weaken in your minds the conviction of this truth : —as this is the point in your [political] fortress against which the batteries of internal and external enemies will be most constantly and actively (though often covertly and insidiously) directed, it is of infinite moment, that you should properly estimate the immense value of your national Union to your collective and individual happiness ;—that you should cherish [†] a cordial, habitual, and immovable attachment [to it, accustoming yourselves to think and speak of it as of the Palladium of your political safety and prosperity ; watching for its preservation with jealous anxiety ; discountenancing whatever may suggest even a suspicion that it can in any event be abandoned, and indignantly frowning upon the first dawning of every attempt to alienate any portion of our country from the rest, or to

* various   † towards it

enfeeble the sacred ties which now link together the various parts.]*

For this you have every inducement of sympathy and interest. Citizens [by birth or choice of a common country],† that country has a right to concentrate your affections. The name of AMERICAN, which belongs to you, in your national capacity, must always exalt the just pride of Patriotism, more than any appellation [‡] derived from local discriminations.— With slight shades of difference, you have the same Religion, Manners, Habits, and political Principles. You have in a common cause fought and triumphed to-

---

* that you should accustom yourselves to reverence it as the Palladium of your political safety and prosperity, adapting constantly your words and actions to that momentous idea ; that you should watch for its preservation with jealous anxiety, discountenance whatever may suggest a suspicion that it can in any event be abandoned ; and frown upon the first dawning of any a'tempt to alienate any portion of our Country from the rest, or to enfeeble the sacred ties which now link together the several parts.

† of a common country by birth or choice
‡ to be

gether. The Independence and Liberty you possess are the work of joint councils and joint efforts—of common dangers, sufferings, and successes.

But these considerations, however powerfully they address themseves to your sensibility, are greatly outweighed by those which apply more immediately to your Interest. Here every portion of our country finds the most commanding motives for carefully guarding and preserving the Union of the whole.

The *North* in an [unrestrained]* intercourse with the *South*, protected by the equal Laws of a common government, finds in the productions of the latter [†] great additional resources of maritime and commercial enterprise—and precious materials of manufacturing industry. The *South*, in the same intercourse benefiting by the agency of the *North*, sees its agriculture grow and its commerce expand. Turning partly into its own channels the seamen of the *North*, it finds its particular

* unfettered   † many of the peculiar

navigation invigorated ; — and while it contributes, in different ways, to nourish and increase the general mass of the national navigation, it looks forward to the protection of a maritime strength to which itself is unequally adapted. The *East*, in a like intercourse with the *West*, already finds, and in the progressive improvement of interior communications, by land and water, will more and more find, a valuable vent for the commodities which it brings from abroad, or manufactures at home. The *West* derives from the *East* supplies requisite to its growth and comfort, and what is perhaps of still greater consequence, it must of necessity owe the *secure* enjoyment of indispensable *outlets* for its own productions to the weight, influence, and the future maritime strength of the Atlantic side of the Union, directed by an indissoluble community of interest, as *one Nation*. [Any other]* tenure by which the *West* can hold this essential advantage, [whether derived] †

* The   † either

from its own separate strength or from an apostate and unnatural connection with any foreign Power, must be intrinsically precarious. [*]

[†]While [then] every part of our country thus [feels] ‡ an immediate and particular interest in Union, all the parts ‖ [combined cannot fail to find] in the united mass of means and efforts [§] greater strength, greater resource, proportionably greater security from external danger, a less frequent interruption of their peace by foreign Nations ; and, [what is] ¶ of inestimable value ! they must derive from Union an exemption from those broils and wars between themselves, which [so frequently] ** afflict neighboring countries, not tied together by the same government ; which their own rivalships alone would be sufficient to produce ; but which oppo-

---

* liable every moment to be disturbed by the fluctuating combinations of the primary interests of Europe, which must be expected to regulate the conduct of the Nations of which it is composed.   † And   ‡ finds   ‖ of it
§ cannot fail to find
¶ which is an advantage   ** inevitably

site foreign alliances, attachments, and
intrigues would stimulate and embitter.
Hence likewise they will avoid the necessity of those overgrown Military establishments, which, under any form of
Government, are inauspicious to liberty,
and which [are to be regarded] * as particularly hostile to Republican Liberty :
In this sense it is, that your Union ought
to be considered as a main prop of your
liberty, and that the love of the one ought
to endear to you the preservation of the
other.

These considerations speak a persuasive
language to [every] † reflecting and virtuous mind,—[and] ‡ exhibit the continuance of the Union as a primary object of
Patriotic desire. Is there a doubt whether
a common government can embrace so
large a sphere ? Let experience solve it.
To listen to mere speculation in such a
case were criminal. [We are authorized]||
to hope that a proper organization of the

* there is reason to regard   † any
‡ they || 'T is natural

whole, with the auxiliary agency of governments for the respective subdivisions, will afford a happy issue to the experiment. 'T is well worth a fair and full experiment. [*] With such powerful and obvious motives to Union, [affecting] † all parts of our country [‡], while experience shall not have demonstrated its impracticability, there will always be [reason] ‖ to distrust the patriotism of those, who in any quarter may endeavour to weaken its bands. [§]

---

* It may not impossibly be found, that the spirit of party, the machinations of foreign powers, the corruption and ambition of individual citizens are more formidable adversaries to the Unity of our Empire than any inherent difficulties in the scheme. Against these the mounds of national opinion, national sympathy, and national jealousy ought to be raised.

† as   ‡ have   ‖ cause in the effect itself

§ Besides the more serious causes already hinted as threatening our Union, there is one less dangerous, but sufficiently dangerous to make it prudent to be upon our guard against it. I allude to the petulance of party differences of opinion. It is not uncommon to hear the irritations which these excite vent themselves in declarations that the different parts of the United States are ill affected to each other, in

In contemplating the causes which may disturb our Union, it occurs as matter of serious concern, that [any ground should have been furnished for characterizing parties by] * *Geographical* discriminations —*Northern* and *Southern*—*Atlantic* and *Western ;* [whence designing men may endeavor to excite a belief that there is a

menaces that the Union will be dissolved by this or that measure. Intimations like these are as indiscreet as they are intemperate. Though frequently made with levity and without any really evil intention, they have a tendency to produce the consequence which they indicate. They teach the minds of men to consider the Union as precarious ;—as an object to which they ought not to attach their hopes and fortunes ;—and thus chill the sentiment in its favor. By alarming the pride of those to whom they are addressed, they set ingenuity at work to depreciate the value of the thing, and to discover reasons of indifference towards it. This is not wise.—It will be much wiser to habituate ourselves to reverence the Union as the palladium of our national happiness ; to accommodate constantly our words and actions to that idea, and to discountenance whatever may suggest a suspicion that it can in any event be abandoned. (In the margin opposite this *paragraph* are the words, " Not important enough.")

* our parties for some time past have been too much characterized by

real difference of local interests and views.]* One of the expedients of Party to acquire influence, within particular districts, is to misrepresent the opinions and aims of other districts. You cannot shield yourselves too much against the jealousies and heartburnings which spring from these misrepresentations. They tend to render alien to each other those who ought to be bound together by fraternal affection. The inhabitants of our western country have lately had a useful lesson on this [head].† They have seen,

---

* These discriminations,————the mere contrivance of the spirit of Party, (always dexterous to seize every handle by which the passions can be wielded, and too skilful not to turn to account the sympathy of neighbourhood), have furnished an argument against the Union as evidence of a real difference of local interests and views; and serve to hazard it by organizing larger districts of country, under the leaders of contending factions; whose rivalships, prejudices, and schemes of ambition, rather than the true interests of the Country, will direct the use of their influence. If it be possible to correct this poison in the habit of our body politic, it is worthy the endeavors of the moderate and the good to affect it.   † subject

in the negotiation by the Executive, and in the unanimous ratification by the Senate, of the Treaty with Spain, and in the universal satisfaction at that event, throughout the United States, a decisive proof how unfounded were the suspicions propagated among them of a policy in the General Government and in the Atlantic States unfriendly to their interests in regard to the MISSISSIPPI. They have been witnesses to the formation of two Treaties, that with G. Britain, and that with Spain, which secure to them every thing they could desire, in respect to our foreign Relations towards confirming their prosperity. Will it not be their wisdom to rely for the preservation of these advantages on the UNION by which they were procured? Will they not henceforth be deaf to those advisers, if such there are, who would sever them from their Brethren, and connect them with Aliens?

To the efficacy and permanency of your Union, a Government for the whole is indispensable. No alliances however strict between the parts can be an adequate substitute. They must inevitably experience the infractions and interruptions which all alliances in all times have experienced. Sensible of this momentous truth, you have improved upon your first essay, by the adoption of a Constitution of Government, better calculated than your former for an intimate Union, and for the efficacious management of your common concerns. This government, the offspring of your own choice, uninfluenced and unawed, adopted upon full investigation and mature deliberation, completely free in its principles, in the distribution of its powers, uniting security with energy, and containing within itself a provision for its own amendment, has a just claim to your confidence and your support. Respect for its authority, compliance with its Laws, acquiescence in its measures, are duties enjoined by the fundamental maxims of true Liberty. The basis of our political systems is the right of the people

to make and to alter their Constitution of
Government. But the Constitution which
at any time exists, 'till changed by an
explicit and authentic act of the whole
People, is sacredly obligatory upon all.
The very idea of the power and the right
of the People to establish Government,
presupposes the duty of every individual
to obey the established Government.

All obstructions to the execution of the
Laws, all combinations and associations,
under whatever plausible character, with
[the real] design to direct, controul,
counteract, or awe the regular deliberation and action of the constituted authori-
ties, are destructive of this fundamental
principle, and of fatal tendency. They
serve to organize faction, to give it an
artificial and extraordinary force—to
put, [*] in the place of the delegated will
of the Nation, the will of a party ; often
a small but artful and enterprising minority of the community ; and, according
to the alternate triumphs of different par-

* it

ties, to make the public administration
the mirror of the ill-concerted and incon-
gruous projects of faction, rather than the
organ of consistent and wholesome plans
digested by common councils and modi-
fied by mutual interests.   However combinations or associations of the above
description may now and then answer
popular ends, [*] they are likely, in the
course of time and things, to become potent
engines, by which cunning, ambitious and
unprincipled men will be enabled to subvert the power of the People, and to usurp
for themselves the reins of Government;
destroying afterwards the very engines
which have lifted them to unjust do-
minion.

Towards the preservation of your Government and the permanency of your
present happy state, it is requisite, not
only that you steadily discountenance ir-
regular opposition to its acknowledged
authority, but also that you resist with
care [the] † spirit of innovation upon its

* and purposes   † a

principles however specious the pretexts.
One method of assault may be to effect,
in the forms of the Constitution, alterations which will impair the energy of the
system, [and thus to] * undermine what
cannot be directly overthrown. In all
the changes to which you may be invited,
remember that time and habit are at least
as necessary to fix the true character of
Governments, as of other human institutions ; that experience is the surest standard by which to test the real tendency
of the existing Constitution of a Country ;
that facility in changes upon the credit
of mere hypothesis and opinion exposes
to perpetual change, from the endless
variety of hypothesis and opinion : and
remember, especially, that for the efficient
management of your common interests in
a country so extensive as ours, a Government of as much vigour as is consistent
with the perfect security of Liberty is indispensable ; Liberty itself will find in
such a Government, with powers properly

* to

distributed and adjusted, its surest guardian. [It is indeed little else than a name, where the Government is too feeble to withstand the enterprises of faction, to confine each member of the Society within the limits prescribed by the laws, and to maintain all in the secure and tranquil enjoyment of the rights of person and property.]*

I have already intimated to you the danger of Parties in the State, with particular reference to the founding of them on Geographical discriminations. Let me now take a more comprehensive view, and warn you in the most solemn manner against the baneful effects of the Spirit of Party, generally.

This Spirit, unfortunately, is inseparable from [our] † nature, having its root in the strongest passions of the [human]

* Owing to you as I do a frank and free disclosure of my heart, I shall not conceal from you the belief I entertain, that your Government as at present constituted is far more likely to prove too feeble than too powerful.
† human

mind. It exists under different shapes in all Governments, more or less stifled, controuled or repressed ; but in those of the popular form it is seen in its greatest rankness, and is truly their worst enemy. *

The alternate domination of one faction over another, sharpened by the spirit of

* In Republics of narrow extent, it is not difficult for those who at any time hold the reins of Power, and command the ordinary public favor, to overturn the established [constitution] * in favor of their own aggrandizement.

The same thing may likewise be too often accomplished in such Republics, by partial combinations of men, who though not in office, from birth, riches or other sources of distinction, have extraordinary influence and numerous [adherents] † By debauching the Military force, by surprising some commanding citadel, or by some other sudden and unforeseen movement the fate of the Republic is decided.—But in Republics of large extent, usurpation can scarcely make its way through these avenues.

The powers and opportunities of resistance of a wide extended and numerous nation, defy the successful efforts of the ordinary Military force, or of any collections which wealth and patronage may call to their aid. In such Republics, it is safe to assert, that the conflicts of popular factions are the chief, if not the only, inlets of usurpation and Tyranny.

* order   † retainers

revenge natural to party dissension, which in different ages and countries has perpetrated the most horrid enormities, is itself a frightful despotism. But this leads at length to a more formal and permanent despotism. The disorders and miseries, which result, gradually incline the minds of men to seek security and repose in the absolute power of an Individual: and sooner or later the chief of some prevailing faction, more able or more fortunate than his own competitors, turns this disposition to the purposes of his own elevation, on the ruins of Public Liberty.

Without looking forward to an extremity of this kind [which nevertheless ought not to be entirely out of sight), the common and continual mischiefs of the spirit of Party are sufficient to make it the interest and the duty of a wise People to discourage and restrain it.

It serves always to distract the Public Councils and enfeeble the Public administration. It agitates the community with ill-founded jealousies and false alarms, kindles the animosity of one part against another, foments occasionally riot and insurrection. It opens the door to foreign influence and corruption, which find a facilitated access [to the Government itself through the channels of party passions. Thus, the policy and the will of one country, are subjected to the policy and will of another.] *

There is an opinion that parties in free countries are useful checks upon the Administration of the Government, and serve to keep alive the Spirit of Liberty. This within certain limits is probably true—and in Governments of a Monarchical cast, Patriotism may look with indulgence, if not with favor, upon the spirit of party. But in those of the popular character, in Governments purely elective, it is a spirit not to be encouraged.

* through the channels of party passions. It frequently subjects the policy of our own country to the policy of some foreign country, and even enslaves the will of our Government to the will of some foreign Government.

From their natural tendency, it is certain
there will always be enough of that spirit
for every salutary purpose,—and there
being constant danger of excess, the
effort ought to be, by force of public
opinion, to mitigate and assuage it. A
fire not to be quenched; it demands a
uniform vigilance to prevent its bursting
into a flame, lest, [instead of warming, it
should]* consume.

It is important, likewise, that the
habits of thinking in a free country
should inspire caution in those entrusted
with its administration, to confine themselves within their respective constitutional spheres; avoiding in the exercise
of the powers of one department to en-
croach upon another. The spirit of en-
croachment tends to consolidate the
powers of all the departments in one, and
thus to create, [†] whatever [the form of
government, a real]‡ despotism. A just
estimate of that love of power, and [||]

* it should not only warm, but
† under   ‡ forms, a || the

proneness to abuse it, which predom-
inates in the human heart, is sufficient to
satisfy us of the truth of this position.
The necessity of reciprocal checks in the
exercise of political power, by dividing
and distributing it into different depos-
itories, and constituting each the Guardian of the Public Weal [against] * invasions by the others, has been evinced by
experiments ancient and modern; some
of them in our own country and under
our own eyes. To preserve them must
be as necessary as to institute them. If
in the opinion of the People, the distribution or modification of the Constitutional
powers be in any particular wrong, let it
be corrected by an amendment in the way
which the Constitution designates. But
let there be no change by usurpation;
for though this, in one instance, may be
the instrument of good, it is the [cus-
tomary] † weapon by which free governments are destroyed. The precedent [‡]
must always greatly overbalance in per-

* from   † usual and natural   ‡ of its use

manent evil any partial or [transient]*
benefit which the use [†] can at any time
yield.

Of all the dispositions and habits which
lead to political prosperity, Religion and
morality are indispensable supports. In
vain would that man claim the tribute of
Patriotism, who should labour to subvert
these great Pillars of human happiness,
these firmest props of the duties of Men
and Citizens. The mere Politician,
equally with the pious man, ought to respect and to cherish them. A volume
could not trace all their connections with
private and public felicity. Let it simply
be asked where is the security for property, for reputation, for life, if the sense
of religious obligation *desert* the oaths,
which are the instruments of investigation in Courts of Justice? And let us
with caution indulge the supposition,
that morality can be maintained without
religion. Whatever may be conceded to
the influence of refined education on

* temporary   † itself

minds of peculiar structure—reason and experience doth forbid us to expect that national morality can prevail in exclusion of religious principle.

'T is substantially true that virtue or morality is a necessary spring of popular government. The rule indeed extends with more or less force to every species of Free Government. Who that is a sincere friend to it, can look with indifference upon attempts to shake the foundation of the fabric?

[Promote then as an object of primary importance, institutions for the general diffusion of knowledge. In proportion as the structure of a government gives force to public opinion, it is essential that public opinion should be enlightened.] *

* Cultivate industry and frugality, as auxiliaries to good morals and sources of private and public prosperity. Is there not room to regret that our propensity to expense exceeds our means for it? Is there not more luxury among us and more diffusively, than suits the actual stage of our national progress? Whatever may be the apology for luxury in a country, mature

As a very important source of strength and security, cherish public credit. One method of preserving it is to use it as [sparingly]* as possible ; avoiding occasions of expense by cultivating peace, but remembering also that timely disbursements to prepare for danger frequently prevent much greater disbursements to repel it—avoiding likewise the accumulation of debt, not only by [shunning]† occasions of expense, but by vigorous exertions in time of Peace to discharge the debts which unavoidable wars may have occasioned, not ungenerously throwing upon posterity the burthen which we ourselves ought to bear. The execution of these maxims belongs to your Representatives, but it is necessary that public opinion should [co-operate.]‡

in the Arts which are its ministers, and the cause of national opulence—can it promote the advantage of a young country, almost wholly agricultural, in the infancy of the Arts, and certainly not in the majority of wealth?

(Over this paragraph in the original a piece of paper is wafered, on which the passage is written as printed in the text.)

* little   † avoiding   ‡ coincide

To facilitate to them the performance of their duty, it is essential that you should practically bear in mind, that towards the payment of debts there must be Revenue—that to have Revenue there must be taxes—that no taxes can be devised which are not more or less inconvenient and unpleasant—that the intrinsic embarrassment inseparable from the selection of the proper objects (which is always a choice of difficulties) ought to be a decisive motive for a candid construction of the conduct of the Government in making it, and for a spirit of acquiescence in the measures for obtaining Revenue which the public exigencies may at any time dictate.

Observe good faith and justice towards all Nations. [*] Cultivate peace and harmony with all. Religion and morality enjoin this conduct; and can it be that good policy does not equally enjoin it? It

* and cultivate peace and harmony with all, for in public as well as in private transactions, I am persuaded that honesty will always be found to be the best policy.

will be worthy of a free, enlightened, and, at no distant period, a great nation, to give to mankind the magnanimous and too novel example of a People always guided by an exalted justice and benevolence. Who can doubt that in the course of time and things, the fruits of such a plan would richly repay any temporary advantages which might be lost by a steady adherence to it? Can it be, that Providence has not connected the permanent felicity of a Nation with its virtue? The experiment, at least, is recommended by every sentiment which ennobles human nature. Alas! is it rendered impossible by its vices?

In the execution of such a plan nothing is more essential than that [permanent, inveterate]* antipathies against particular nations and passionate attachments for others should be excluded ; and that in place of them just and amicable feelings towards all should be cultivated. The Nation, which indulges towards another

* rooted

[an]* habitual hatred or [an]† habitual fondness, is in some degree a slave. It is a slave to its animosity or to its affection, either of which is sufficient to lead it astray from its duty and its interests. Antipathy in one Nation against another [‡] disposes each more readily to offer insult and injury, to lay hold of slight causes of umbrage, and to be haughty and intractable, when accidental or trifling occasions of dispute occur. Hence frequent collisions, obstinate, envenomed and bloody contests. The Nation prompted by ill-will and resentment sometimes impels to War the Government, contrary to [the best] || calculations of policy. The Government sometimes participates in the [national] propensity, and adopts through passion what reason would reject ; at other times, it makes the animosity of the Nation subservient to projects of hostility instigated by pride. ambition, and other sinister and perni-

---

* a   † a
‡ begets of course a similar sentiment in that other, || its own

cious motives. The peace, often sometimes perhaps the Liberty, of Nations has been the victim.

So likewise a passionate attachment of one Nation for another produces a variety of evils. Sympathy for the favourite nation, facilitating the illusion of an imaginary common interest in case where no common interest exists, and infusing into one [*] the enmities of the other, betrays the former into a participation in the quarrels and wars of the latter, without adequate inducement or justification : It leads also to concessions to the favourite Nation of privileges denied to others, which is apt doubly to injure the Nation making the concessions ; [†] by unnecessarily parting ,with what ought to have been retained,‡ and by exciting jealousy, ill-will, and a disposition to retaliate in the parties from whom equal privileges are withheld ; and it gives to ambitious, corrupted, or deluded citizens (who devote themselves to the favourite Nation)

* another   † 1stly   ‡ 2dly

facility to betray, or sacrifice the interests of their own country without odium, sometimes even with popularity : gilding with the appearances of a virtuous sense of obligation, a commendable deference for public opinion, or a laudable zeal for public good, the base or foolish compliances of ambition, corruption, or infatuation.

As avenues to foreign influence in innumerable ways, such attachments are particularly alarming to the truly enlightened and independent patriot. How many opportunities do they afford to tamper with domestic factions, to practise the arts of seduction, to mislead public opinion, to influence or awe the public councils ! Such an attachment of a small or weak, towards a great and powerful nation, dooms the former to be the satellite of the latter.

Against the insidious wiles of foreign influence, [I conjure you to] believe me, [fellow citizens],* the jealousy of a free
* my friends

people ought to be [constantly]* awake, since history and experience prove that foreign influence is one of the most baneful foes of Republican Government. But that jealousy to be useful must be impartial ; else it becomes the instrument of the very influence to be avoided, instead of a defence against it. Excessive partiality for one foreign nation and excessive dislike of another, cause those whom they actuate to see danger only on one side, and serve to veil and even second the arts of influence on the other. Real Patriots, who may resist the intrigues of the favourite, are liable to become suspected and odious ; while its tools and dupes usurp the applause and confidence of the people, to surrender their interests.

The great rule of conduct for us, in regard to foreign Nations is, [in extending our commercial relations,] to have with them as little *Political* connection as possible. So far as we have already formed engagements let them be fulfilled

* incessantly

with [*] perfect good faith. Here let us stop.

Europe has a set of primary interests, which to us have none, or a very remote relation. Hence she must be engaged in frequent controversies, the causes of which are essentially foreign to our concerns. Hence therefore it must be unwise in us to implicate ourselves by [†] artificial [ties] ‡ in the ordinary vicissitudes of her politics, [or] || the ordinary combinations and collisions of her friendships, or enmities.

Our detached and distant situation invites and enables us to pursue a different course. If we remain one People, under an efficient government, the period is not far off, when we may defy material injury from external annoyance ; when we take such an attitude as will cause the neutrality we may at any time resolve [upon] § to be scrupulously respected. When [¶]

---

* circumspection indeed, but with   † an
‡ connection || in   § to observe
¶ neither of two

belligerent nations, under the impossibility of making acquisitions upon us, will [not] lightly hazard the giving us provocation [*]; when we may choose peace or war, as our interest guided by [†] justice shall counsel.

Why forego the advantages of so peculiar a situation? Why quit our own to stand upon foreign ground? Why, by interweaving our destiny with that of any part of Europe, entangle our peace and prosperity in the toils of European ambition, rivalship, interest, humour, or caprice?

'T is our true policy to steer clear of permanent alliances [‡] with any portion of the foreign world;—so far, I mean, as we are now at liberty to do it—for let me not be understood as capable of patronizing infidelity to [existing]|| engagements, ([I hold the maxim no less applicable to public than to private affairs],§ that hon-

---

* to throw our weight into the opposite scale;
† our   ‡ intimate connections || pre-ëxisting
§ for I hold it to be as true in public as in private transactions,

esty is [always] the best policy). [I repeat it therefore let those engagements] * be observed in their genuine sense. But in my opinion it is unnecessary and would be unwise to extend them.

Taking care always to keep ourselves, by suitable establishments, on a respectably defensive posture, we may safely trust to [temporary] † alliances for extraordinary emergencies.

Harmony, liberal intercourse with all nations, are recommended by policy, humanity, and interest. But even our commercial policy should hold an equal and impartial hand: neither seeking nor granting exclusive favours and preferences; consulting the natural course of things; diffusing and diversifying by gentle means the streams of commerce, but forcing nothing; establishing with Powers so disposed—in order to give to trade a stable course, to define the rights of our Merchants and to enable the Government to support them—conventional rules of

* those must † occasional

intercourse, the best that present circumstances and mutual opinion will permit; but temporary, and liable to be from time to time abandoned or varied, as experience and circumstances shall dictate; constantly keeping in view, that 't is folly in one nation to look for disinterested favors [from] * another; that it must pay with a portion of its independence for whatever it may accept under that character—that by such acceptance it may place itself in the condition of having given equivalents for nominal favours and yet of being reproached with ingratitude for not giving more. There can be no greater error than to expect, or calculate upon real favors from Nation to Nation. 'T is an illusion which experience must cure, which a just pride ought to discard.

In offering to you, my Countrymen, these counsels of an old and affectionate friend, I dare not hope they will make the strong and lasting impression I could wish; that they will control the usual

* at

current of the passions or prevent our
nation from running the course which
has hitherto marked the destiny of Nations. But if I may even flatter myself,
that they may be productive of some partial benefit ; some occasional good ; that
they may now and then recur to moderate the fury of party spirit, to warn against
the mischiefs of foreign intrigue, to guard
against the impostures of pretended patriotism, this hope will be a full recom-
pense for the solicitude for your welfare,
by which they have been dictated.

How far in the discharge of my official
duties I have been guided by the principles which have been delineated, the public Records and other evidences of my
conduct must witness to You, and to the
World. To myself, the assurance of my
own conscience is, that I have at least
believed myself to be guided by them.

In relation to the still subsisting War
in Europe, my Proclamation of the 22d
of April, 1793, is the index to my plan.
Sanctioned by your approving voice and

by that of Your Representatives in both Houses of Congress, the spirit of that measure has continually governed me : uninfluenced by any attempts to deter or divert me from it.

After deliberate examination with the aid of the best lights I could obtain, [*] I was well satisfied that our country, under all the circumstances of the case, had a right to take, and was bound in duty and interest, to take a Neutral position. Having taken it, I determined, as far as should depend upon me, to maintain it, with moderation, perseverance, and firmness.

[The considerations which respect the right to hold this conduct, [it is not necessary] † on this occasion [to detail]. I will only observe, that according to my understanding of the matter, that right, so far from being denied by any of the Bel-

(* and from men disagreeing in their impressions of the origin, progress, and nature of that war,)

† some of them of a delicate nature, would be improperly the subject of explanation.

ligerent Powers, has been virtually admitted by all.] *

The duty of holding a neutral conduct may be inferred, without any thing more, from the obligation which justice and humanity impose on every Nation, in cases in which it is free to act, to maintain inviolate the relations of Peace and Amity towards other Nations.

* The considerations which respect the right to hold this conduct, some of them of a delicate nature, would be improperly the subject of explanation on this occasion. I will barely observe that according to my understanding of the matter, that right so far from being denied by any belligerent Power, has been virtually admitted by all.

(This paragraph is then erased from the word "conduct," and the following sentence interlined : "would be improperly the subject of particular discussion on this occasion. I will barely observe that to me they appear to be warranted by well-established principles of the Laws of Nations as applicable to the nature of our alliance with France in connection with the circumstances of the War and the relative situation of the contending Parties."

A piece of paper is afterwards wafered over both, on which the paragraph as it stands in the text is written, and on the margin is the following note : " This is the first draft, and it is questionable which of the two is to be preferred.")

The inducements of interest for observing that conduct, will best be referred to your own reflections and experience. With me, a predominant motive has been to endeavour to gain time to our country to settle and mature its yet recent institutions, and to progress without interruption to that degree of strength and consistency, which is necessary to give it, humanly speaking, the command of its own fortunes.

Though in reviewing the incidents of my Administration, I am unconscious of intentional error—I am nevertheless too sensible of my defects not to think it probable that I [may] have committed many errors. [Whatever they may be I]* fervently beseech the Almighty to avert or mitigate [the evils to which they may tend.] † I shall also carry with me the hope that my country will never cease to view them with indulgence ; and that after forty-five years of my life dedicated

*I deprecate the evils to which they may tend, and   †them

to its service, with an upright zeal, the faults of incompetent abilities will be consigned to oblivion, as myself must soon be to the mansions of rest. [*]

Relying on its kindness in this as in other things, and actuated by that fervent love towards it, which is so natural to a man, who views in it the native soil of himself and his progenitors for [several] †

* May I without the charge of ostentation add, that neither ambition nor interest has been the impelling cause of my actions—that I have never designedly misused any power confided to me nor hesitated to use one, where I thought it could redound to your benefit? May I without the appearance of affectation say, that the fortune with which I came into office is not bettered otherwise than by the improvement in the value of property which the quick progress and uncommon prosperity of our country have produced? May I still further add without breach of delicacy, that I shall retire without cause for a blush, with no sentiments alien to the force of those vows for the happiness of his country so natural to a citizen who sees in it the native soil of his progenitors and himself for four generations?

(On the margin opposite this paragraph is the following note : " This paragraph may have the appearance of self-distrust and mere vanity.")

* four

generations ; I anticipate with pleasing expectation that retreat, in which I promise myself to realize, without alloy, the sweet enjoyment of partaking in the midst of my fellow citizens, the benign influence of good Laws under a free Government, the ever favourite object of my heart, and the happy reward, as I trust, of our mutual cares, labours, and dangers.*

GEO. WASHINGTON.

UNITED STATES,
  19*th September*, } 1796.

(* The paragraph beginning with the words, "May I without the charge of ostentation add," having been struck out, the following note is written on the margin of that which is inserted in its place in the text: "Continuation of the paragraph preceding the last ending with the word 'rest.' ")

LINCOLN'S INAUGURAL
ADDRESS

A. Lincoln

INAUGURAL ADDRESS.

———

MARCH 4, 1861.

FELLOW-CITIZENS of the United States.—In compliance with a custom as old as the government itself, I appear before you to address you briefly, and to take in your presence the oath prescribed by the Constitution of the United States to be taken by the President "before he enters on the execution of his office."

I do not consider it necessary at present for me to discuss those matters of administration about which there is no special anxiety or excitement.

Apprehension seems to exist, among the people of the Southern States, that by the accession of a Republican administration their property and their peace and personal security are to be endangered. There never has been any reasonable cause for such apprehension. Indeed, the most ample evidence to the contrary has all the while existed and been open to their inspection. It is found in nearly all the published speeches of him who now addresses you. I do but quote from one of those speeches when I declare that " I have no purpose, directly or indirectly, to interfere with the institution of slavery in the States where it exists. I believe I have no lawful right to do so, and I have no inclination to do so." Those who nominated and elected me did so with full knowledge that I had made this and many similar declarations, and had never recanted them. And more than this, they placed in the platform for my acceptance, and as a law to themselves and to me, the clear and emphatic resolution which I now read :

" *Resolved*, That the maintenance inviolate of the rights of the States, and especially the right of each State to order and control its own domestic institutions according to its judgment exclusively, is essential to the balance of power on which the perfection and endurance of our political fabric depend, and we denounce the lawless invasion by armed force of the soil of any State or Territory, no matter under what pretext, as among the gravest of crimes.''

I now reiterate these sentiments; and, in doing so, I only impress upon the public attention the most conclusive evidence of which the case is susceptible, that the property, peace, and security of no section are to be in any wise endangered by the now incoming administration. I add, too, that all the protection which, consistently with the Constitution and the laws, can be given, will be cheerfully given to all the States, when lawfully demanded, for whatever cause, as cheerfully to one section as to another.

There is much controversy about the

delivering up of fugitives from service or labor. The clause I now read is as plainly written in the Constitution as any other of its provisions:

"No person held to service or labor in one State, under the laws thereof, escaping into another, shall, in consequence of any law or regulation therein, be discharged from such service or labor, but shall be delivered up on claim of the party to whom such service or labor may be due."

It is scarcely questioned that this provision was intended by those who made it for the reclaiming of what we call fugitive slaves; and the intention of the lawgiver is the law. All members of Congress swear their support to the whole Constitution—to this provision as much as any other. To the proposition, then, that slaves whose cases come within the terms of this clause, "shall be delivered up," their oaths are unanimous. Now, if they would make the effort in good temper, could they not, with nearly equal unanimity, frame and pass a law by means of which to keep good that unanimous oath?

There is some difference of opinion whether this clause should be enforced by National or by State authority; but surely that difference is not a very material one. If the slave is to be surrendered, it can be of but little consequence to him, or to others, by what authority it is done. And should any one, in any case, be content that his oath should go unkept, on a mere unsubstantial controversy as to how it shall be kept?

Again, in any law upon this subject, ought not all the safeguards of liberty known in civilized and humane jurisprudence to be introduced, so that a free man be not, in any case, surrendered as a slave? And might it not be well, at the same time, to provide by law for the enforcement of that clause of the Constitution which guarantees that " the citizens of each State shall be entitled to all privileges and immunities of citizens in the several States " ?

I take the official oath to-day with no mental reservation, and with no purpose to construe the Constitution or laws by any hypercritical rules. And while I do not choose now to specify particular acts of Congress as proper to be enforced, I do suggest that it will be much safer for all, both in official and private stations, to conform to and abide by all those acts which stand unrepealed, than to violate any of them, trusting to find impunity in having them held to be unconstitutional.

It is seventy-two years since the first inauguration of a President under our National Constitution. During that period, fifteen different and greatly distinguished citizens have, in succession, administered the Executive branch of the government. They have conducted it through many perils, and generally with great success. Yet, with all this sccpe for precedent, I now enter upon the same task for the brief constitutional term of four years, under great and peculiar difficulty. A disruption of the Federal Union, heretofore only menaced, is now formidably attempted.

I hold that in contemplation of universal law, and of the Constitution, *the Union of these States is perpetual.* Perpetuity is implied, if not expressed, in the fundamental law of all national governments. It is safe to assert that no government proper ever had a provision in its organic law for its own termination. Continue to execute all the express provisions of our National Government, and the Union will endure forever—it being impossible to destroy it, except by some action not provided for in the instrument itself.

Again, if the United States be not a government proper, but an association of States in the nature of contract merely, can it, as a contract, be peaceably unmade by less than all the parties who made it? One party to a contract may violate it— break it, so to speak; but does it not require all to lawfully rescind it?

Descending from these general principles, we find the proposition that, in legal contemplation, the Union is perpetual, confirmed by the history of the Union itself. The Union is much older than the Constitution. It was formed, in fact, by the Articles of Association in 1774. It was matured and continued by the Declaration of Independence in 1776. It was further matured, and the faith of all the then thirteen States expressly plighted and engaged that it should be perpetual, by the Articles of Confederation in 1778. And, finally, in 1787, one of the declared objects for ordaining and establishing the Constitution was " to form a more perfect union."

But if destruction of the Union, by one, or by a part only, of the States, be lawfully possible, the Union is less perfect than before, the Constitution having lost the vital element of perpetuity.

It follows, from these views, that no State, upon its own mere motion, can lawfully get out of the Union ; that resolves and ordinances to that effect are legally void ; and that acts of violence within any State or States, against the authority of the United States, are insurrectionary or revolutionary, according to circumstances.

I therefore consider that, in view of the Constitution and the laws, the Union is unbroken, and to the extent of my ability I shall take care, as the Constitution itself expressly enjoins upon me, that the laws of the Union be faithfully executed in all the States. Doing this I deem to be only a simple duty on my part ; and I shall perform it, so far as practicable, unless my rightful masters, the American people, shall withhold the requisite means, or, in some authoritative manner, direct the contrary. I trust this will not be regarded as a menace, but only as the declared purpose of the Union that it will constitutionally defend and maintain itself. In doing this there need be no bloodshed or violence ; and there shall be none, unless it be forced upon the National authority. The power confided to me will be used to hold, occupy, and possess the property and places belonging to the government, and to collect the duties and imposts; but beyond what may be necessary for these objects, there will be no invasion, no using of force against or among the people anywhere. Where hostility to the United States, in any interior locality, shall be so great and universal as to prevent competent resident citizens from holding the Federal offices, there will be no attempt to force obnoxious strangers among the people for that object. While the strict legal right may exist in the government to enforce the exercise of these offices, the attempt to do so would be so irritating, and so nearly impracticable withal, that I deem it better to forego, for the time, the uses of such offices.

The mails, unless repelled, will continue to be furnished in all parts of the Union. So far as possible, the people everywhere shall have that sense of perfect security which is most favorable to calm thought and reflection. The course here indicated will be followed, unless current events and experience shall show a modification or change to be proper, and in every case and exigency my best discretion will be exercised, according to circumstances actually existing, and with a view and a hope of a peaceful solution of the National troubles, and the restoration of fraternal sympathies and affections.

That there are persons in one section or another who seek to destroy the Union at all events, and are glad of any pretext to do it, I will neither affirm nor deny ; but if there be such, I need address no word to them. To those, however, who really love the Union, may I not speak ?

Before entering upon so grave a matter as the destruction of our National fabric, with all its benefits, its memories, and its hopes, would it not be wise to ascertain why we do it ? Will you hazard so desperate a step while there is any possibility that any portion of the certain ills

you fly from have no real existence? Will
you, while the certain ills you fly to are
greater than all the real ones you fly from,
—will you risk the commission of so fear-
ful a mistake?

All profess to be content in the Union,
if all constitutional rights can be maintained. Is it true, then, that any right,
plainly written in the Constitution, has
been denied? I think not. Happily the
human mind is so constituted that no
party can reach to the audacity of doing
this. Think, if you can, of a single instance in which a plainly written provision of the Constitution has ever been
denied. If, by the mere force of numbers, a majority should deprive a minority
of any clearly written constitutional right,
it might, in a moral point of view, justify
revolution—certainly would if such right
were a vital one. But such is not our
case. All the vital rights of minorities
and of individuals are so plainly assured
to them by affirmations and negations,
guaranties and prohibitions in the Con-

stitution, that controversies never arise concerning them. But no organic law can ever be framed with a provision specifically applicable to every question which may occur in practical administration. No foresight can anticipate, nor any document of reasonable length contain, express provisions for all possible questions. Shall fugitives from labor be surrendered by National or State authority? The Constitution does not expressly say. May Congress prohibit slavery in the Territories? The Constitution does not expressly say. Must Congress protect slavery in the Territories? The Constitution does not expressly say.

From questions of this class spring all our constitutional controversies, and we divide upon them into majorities and minorities. If the minority will not acquiesce, the majority must, or the government must cease. There is no other alternative; for continuing the government is acquiescence on one side or the other. If a minority in such case will secede rather than acquiesce, they make a precedent which, in turn, will divide and ruin them; for a minority of their own will secede from them whenever a majority refuses to be controlled by such a minority. For instance, why may not any portion of a new confederacy, a year or two hence, arbitrarily secede again, precisely as portions of the present Union now claim to secede from it? All who cherish disunion sentiments are now being educated to the exact temper of doing this.

Is there such perfect identity of interests among the States to compose a new Union, as to produce harmony only, and prevent renewed secession?

Plainly, the central idea of secession is the essence of anarchy. A majority held in restraint by constitutional checks and limitations, and always changing easily with deliberate changes of popular opinions and sentiments, is the only true sovereign of a free people. Whoever rejects it, does, of necessity, fly to anarchy or to despotism. Unanimity is impossible ; the rule of a minority, as a permanent arrangement, is wholly inadmissible ; so that, rejecting the majority principle, anarchy or despotism, in some form, is all that is left. . . .

Physically speaking, we cannot separate. We cannot remove our respective sections from each other, nor build an impassable wall between them. A husband and wife may be divorced, and go out of the presence and beyond the reach of each other ; but the different parts of our country cannot do this. They cannot but remain face to face, and intercourse, either amicable or hostile, must continue between them. It is impossible, then, to make that intercourse more advantageous or more satisfactory after separation than before. Can aliens make treaties easier than friends can make laws? Can treaties be more faithfully enforced between aliens than laws can among friends? Suppose you go to war, you cannot fight always, and when after much loss on both sides and no gain on either you cease fighting, the identical old questions as to terms of intercourse are again upon you.

This country, with its institutions, belongs to the people who inhabit it. Whenever they shall grow weary of the existing government they can exercise their constitutional right of amending it, or their revolutionary right to dismember or overthrow it. I cannot be ignorant of the fact that many worthy and patriotic citizens are desirous of having the National Constitution amended. . . . I understand a proposed amendment to the Constitution — which amendment, however, I have not seen—has passed Congress, to the effect that the Federal Government shall never interfere with the domestic institutions of the States, including that of persons held to service. To avoid misconstruction of what I have said, I depart from my purpose not to speak of particular amendments, so far as to say that, holding such a provision now to be implied constitutional law, I have no objections to its being made express and irrevocable.

The Chief Magistrate derives all his authority from the people, and they have conferred none upon him to fix terms for the separation of the States. The people themselves can do this also if they choose, but the Executive, as such, has nothing to do with it. His duty is to administer the present government as it came to his hands, and to transmit it, unimpaired by him, to his successor. Why should there not be a patient confidence in the ultimate justice of the people? Is there any better or equal hope in the world? In our present differences is either party without faith of being in the right? If the Almighty Ruler of Nations, with His eternal truth and justice, be on your side of the North, or yours of the South, that truth and that justice will surely prevail, by the judgment of this great tribunal of the American people. By the frame of the Government under which we live, the same people have wisely given their public servants but little power for mischief, and have with equal wisdom provided for the return of that little to their own hands at very short intervals. While the people retain their virtue and vigilance, no administration, by any extreme of wickedness or folly, can very seriously injure the government in the short space of four years.

My countrymen, one and all, think calmly and well upon this whole subject. Nothing valuable can be lost by taking time. If there be an object to hurry any of you in hot haste to a step which you would never take deliberately, that object will be frustrated by taking time; but no good object can be frustrated by it. Such of you as are now dissatisfied still have the old Constitution unimpaired, and on the sensitive point, the laws of your own framing under it; while the new administration will have no immediate power, if it would, to change either. If it were admitted that you who are dissatisfied hold the right side in this dispute, there is still no single good reason for precipitate action. Intelligence, patriotism, Christianity, and a firm reliance on Him who has never yet forsaken this favored land are still competent to adjust in the best way all our present difficulty. In your hands, my dissatisfied fellow-countrymen, and not in mine, are the momentous issues of civil war. The government will not assail you. You can have no conflict without being yourselves the aggressors. You have no oath registered in Heaven to destroy the government, while I shall have the most solemn one to "preserve, protect, and defend" it.

I am loth to close. We are not enemies, but friends. We must not be enemies. Though passion may have strained, it must not break, our bonds of affection. The mystic chords of memory, stretching from every battle-field and patriot grave to every living heart and hearthstone all over this broad land, will yet swell the chorus of the Union when again touched, as surely they will be, by the better angels of our nature.

LINCOLN'S SECOND INAUGURAL ADDRESS

SECOND INAUGURAL ADDRESS.

MARCH 4, 1865.

FELLOW-COUNTRYMEN.—At this second appearing to take the oath of the Presidential office, there is less occasion for an extended address than there was at first. Then a statement, somewhat in detail, of a course to be pursued seemed very fitting and proper. Now, at the expiration of four years, during which public declarations have been constantly called forth on every point and phase of the great contest which still absorbs the attention and engrosses the energies of the nation, little that is new could be presented.

The progress of our arms, upon which all else chiefly depends, is as well known to the public as to myself, and it is, I trust, reasonably satisfactory and encouraging to all. With high hope for the future, no prediction in regard to it is ventured.

On the occasion corresponding to this four years ago, all thoughts were anxiously directed to an impending civil war. All dreaded it, all sought to avoid it. While the inaugural address was being delivered from this place, devoted altogether to saving the Union without war, insurgent agents were in the city seeking to destroy it with war—seeking to dissolve the Union and divide the effects by negotiation. Both parties deprecated war, but one of them would make war rather than let the nation survive, and the other would accept war rather than let it perish, and the war came. One eighth of the whole population were colored slaves, not distributed generally over the Union, but localized in the Southern part of it. These slaves constituted a peculiar and powerful interest.

All knew that this interest was somehow the cause of the war. To strengthen, perpetuate, and extend this interest was the object for which the insurgents would rend the Union by war, while the government claimed no right to do more than to restrict the territorial enlargement of it.

Neither party expected for the war the magnitude or the duration which it has already attained. Neither anticipated that the cause of the conflict might cease when, or even before the conflict, itself should cease. Each looked for an easier triumph, and a result less fundamental and astounding. Both read the same Bible and pray to the same God, and each invokes His aid against the other. It may seem strange that any men should dare to ask a just God's assistance in wringing their bread from the sweat of other men's faces, but let us judge not, that we be not judged. The prayer of both could not be answered. That of neither has been answered fully. The

Almighty has His own purposes. "Woe unto the world because of offences, for it must needs be that offences come, but woe to that man by whom the offence cometh!" If we shall suppose that American slavery is one of those offences which, in the providence of God, must needs come, but which having continued through His appointed time, He now wills to remove, and that He gives to both North and South this terrible war as the woe due to those by whom the offence came, shall we discern there any departure from those Divine attributes which the believers in a living God always ascribe to Him? Fondly do we hope, fervently do we pray, that this mighty scourge of war may speedily pass away. Yet if God wills that it continue until all the wealth piled by the bondsman's two hundred and fifty years of unrequited toil shall be sunk, and until every drop of blood drawn with the lash shall be paid by another drawn with the sword, as was said three thousand years ago, so still it must be said, that the judgments of the Lord are true and righteous altogether.

With malice toward none, with charity for all, with firmness in the right as God gives us to see the right, let us finish the work we are in, to bind up the nation's wounds, to care for him who shall have borne the battle, and for his widow and his orphans, to do all which may achieve and cherish a just and a lasting peace among ourselves and with all nations.

LINCOLN'S GETTYSBURG ADDRESS

THE GETTYSBURG ADDRESS.

NOVEMBER 19, 1863.

FOURSCORE and seven years ago our fathers brought forth upon this continent a new nation, conceived in liberty, and dedicated to the proposition that all men are created equal. Now we are engaged in a great civil war, testing whether that nation, or any nation so conceived and so dedicated, can long endure. We are met on a great battle-field of that war. We have come to dedicate a portion of that field as a final resting-place for those who here gave their lives that that nation might live. It is altogether fitting and proper that we should do this. But in a larger sense we cannot dedicate, we cannot consecrate, we cannot hallow this ground. The brave men, living and

dead, who struggled here, have conse-
crated it far above our power to add or
detract. The world will little note, nor
long remember, what we say here, but it
can never forget what they did here. It is
for us, the living, rather to be dedicated
here to the unfinished work which they
who fought here have thus far so nobly
advanced. It is rather for us to be here
dedicated to the great task remaining
before us, that from these honored dead
we take increased devotion to that cause
for which they gave the last full measure
of devotion ; that we here highly resolve
that these dead shall not have died in
vain ; that this nation, under God, shall
have a new birth of freedom, and that
government of the people, by the people,
and for the people, shall not perish from
the earth.

APPENDIX

APPENDIX.

DECLARATION OF INDEPENDENCE.

The resolution for Independence was introduced by Richard Henry Lee in the Continental Congress on June 7, 1776. For two days it was discussed by that body, which then deferred further consideration till July 2d, in order to give the colonies that had not yet instructed their delegations to vote for it, time to do so; but that no time might be lost, a committee, consisting of Thomas Jefferson, John Adams, Benjamin Franklin, Roger Sherman, and Robert R. Livingston was appointed to prepare a declaration.

On July 2d the Continental Congress "*Re·solved*, That these United Colonies are, and of right ought to be, Free and Independent States;

and that they are absolved from all allegiance to the British crown, and that political connection between them and the state of Great Britain is, and ought to be, totally dissolved,"—and this is the true " Declaration of Independence."

The resolution, however, needed justification ; and what has therefore since been known as the Declaration of Independence was drawn by Thomas Jefferson, and after slight alterations by the Committee and by the Congress, was published to the world by the latter as their reasons and justification for the original resolution, and as a mutual pledge by the members of life, fortune, and honor to support the measure, by the signing of which, each man, so far as Great Britain was concerned, declared himself a traitor ; so that Franklin laughingly remarked that they must all hang together, or they would all hang separately.

CONSTITUTION.

The Constitution of the United States was framed by a Convention of delegates from the thirteen original States (Rhode Island excepted) which assembled at Philadelphia in May, 1787, and adjourned in September of the same year. By this Convention the Constitution was transmitted to the Continental Congress, who referred it to the State legislatures, which agreeably to the advice of the Federal Convention, called State conventions to consider and ratify or reject. The State conventions adopted it in the following order : Delaware, December 7, 1787; Pennsylvania, December 12, 1787; New Jersey, December 18, 1787 ; Georgia, January 2, 1788 ; Connecticut, January 9, 1788 ; Massachusetts, February 6, 1788 ; Maryland, April 28, 1788; South Carolina, May 23, 1788 ; and New Hampshire, June 21, 1788. By the final clause of the Constitution, it was to be established when nine States should accept it, so with this ratification by New Hampshire, it became the supreme law of the land, so far as the adopting States were concerned. The other States ratified it as follows : Virginia, June 26, 1788 ; New York, July 26, 1788 ; North Carolina, November 21, 1788 ; Rhode Island, May 29, 1790.

WASHINGTON'S CIRCULAR LETTER.

The signing of the definitive treaty of peace with Great Britain, left the United States with a comparatively large unpaid, and dissatisfied army, an empty treasury, and a weak government. Outspoken discontent was prevalent among the troops, who even talked of obtaining justice from the Congress by the bayonet. The States refused all money or other aid to the Continental Congress, which was practically without power to enforce its resolves. Rumors of a military conspiracy to overturn the present government were whispered about, and it was stated that Washington was to be king. All this fiction was destroyed by his voluntarily resigning his commission; but even before this, Washington sent forth this circular letter to the Governors of the States, in which he not only announces his retirement into private life, but points out the evils and weakness of the general government, and the necessity for a general change. Believing, as he did, that he was retiring to Mount Vernon for the rest of his life, it practically is his first farewell address to the States and people.

WASHINGTON'S FIRST INAUGURAL ADDRESS.

The Constitution having been ratified by the necessary number of States in June, 1788, the Continental Congress appointed the first Wednesday, in January, 1789, the day for the choosing of Presidential electors, and the 4th of March in the same year the date for the assembling of the new Congress. The Congress did not succeed in organizing till April 6th however, when an examination of the electoral vote showed George Washington to have been unanimously elected President. Being duly notified of this, he left Mount Vernon on April 16th, reaching New York on the 23d of the same month.

On the 30th of April he attended the Congress, and having first taken the oath of office in sight of the people on the balcony of the Federal Hall, he returned to the Senate Chamber and read this first inaugural address, a contemporary account of the delivery of which has been left us by Senator Maclay : " As the company returned into the Chamber the President took the chair, and the Senate and Representatives their seats. He arose, and all arose, and he addressed them. This great man was agitated and embarrassed more than ever he was by the levelled cannon or pointed musket. He trembled, and several times could scarce make out to read, though it must be supposed he had often read it before. He made a flourish with his right hand which left rather an ungainly impression. I sincerely, for my part, wish all set ceremony in the hands of the dancing masters, and that this first of men had read off his address in the plainest manner, without ever taking his eyes from the paper; for I felt hurt that he was not first in every thing."

WASHINGTON'S SECOND INAUGURAL ADDRESS.

To understand the brevity of Washington's Second Inaugural Address (page 99), it must be remembered that at the time it was considered in the light of a verbal message to Congress, rather than as a statement of facts and policy to the people. As such it was delivered before the Senate, convened for that day only, and was given to the public in the proceedings of that body.

But there was an additional reason for the shortness of this particular address. The Democratic party, then just organizing, had already begun its attacks on Washington. "The Federalists are Monarchists; Washington is their leader. Therefore Washington is aiming to be king." Such was the tendency, if not the direct argument, of the opposition. The mere motion for the House of Representatives to adjourn on February 22d, in order that the members might pay calls of respect on Washington, met with factious opposition, as an improper attention to pay to the man, and any other approach to the slightest form or ceremony was hailed by the Democratic press and politicians as another step towards the monarchy that was then such a *bête noire*.

Thus there was not only the question whether a public inauguration was necessary, but also, whether it would be policy to give the opposition a possible chance of attack by making it so. Washington therefore hesitated, and finally on the 27th of February called a Cabinet council, and requested a written opinion on the

question. Hamilton, for "prudential considerations," advised that the oath be taken at his
own house, and in this Jefferson concurred.
Knox and Randolph, on the contrary, advised
that it be taken in the Senate-chamber, but
were careful to recommend that he "go without
form, attended by such gentlemen as he may
choose, and return without form, except that
he be preceded by the marshal"; and Washington took the second course, but as the
opinions were not given till March 1st, little
time was left to prepare the inaugural address.

Arthur J. Stansbury has left what purported
to be recollections of the delivery of this second
inaugural address, which have been used by both
Schroeder and Lossing in their biographies of
Washington, but a cursory examination of the
statements shows that the account refers to
Washington's address to Congress in November, 1793, and not to this second inaugural
address.

WASHINGTON'S FAREWELL ADDRESS.

In 1792, near the expiration of Washington's
first term, he seriously thought of retiring from

the presidency, and so obtained from James Madison his ideas of what should be touched upon in a farewell address. Over-persuaded by his friends and political advisers he was induced to continue in office, only to repent " once having slipped the moment of resigning his office, and that was every moment since," and to become the subject of such bitter and partisan attacks that a large body of the people were alienated from him and his position made extremely distasteful to him. Thus, when a second opportunity arrived of retiring from the public service he seized upon it, and having consulted and received aid from Alexander Hamilton and John Jay in the preparation of this Farewell Address, he issued it to the people as an announcement of his intention, and as a beacon light for their future political guidance.

PAUL LEICESTER FORD.

BROOKLYN,
March 30, 1889.

INDEX TO THE CONSTITUTION

INDEX TO THE CONSTITUTION.

Knickerbocker Nuggets.

NUGGET—"A diminutive mass of precious metal."

"Little gems of bookmaking."—*Commercial Gazette*, Cincinnati.

"For many a long day nothing has been thought out or worked out so sure to prove entirely pleasing to cultured book-lovers."—*The Bookmaker.*

I—Gesta Romanorum. Tales of the old monks. Edited by C. SWAN . . . $1 00

"This little gem is a collection of stories composed by the monks of old, who were in the custom of relating them to each other after meals for their mutual amusement and information."—*Williams' Literary Monthly.*

"Nuggets indeed, and charming ones, are these rescued from the mine of old Latin, which would certainly have been lost to many busy readers who can only take what comes to them without delvi ʳ for hidden treasures."

II—Headlɯng Hall and Nightmare Abbey. By THOMAS LOᵛ PEACOCK . . . $1 00

"It must haᵥ ˒ court librarian of King Oberon who originally orueɪ ˍ series of quaintly artistic little volumes that Messrs. Putnam are publishing under the name of Knickerbocker Nuggets. There is an elfin dignity in the aspect of these books in their bindings of dark and light blue with golden arabesques."—*Portland Press.*

III—Gulliver's Travels. By JONATHAN SWIFT. A reprint of the early complete edition. Very fully illustrated. Two vols. $2 50

"Messrs. Putnam have done a substantial service to all readers of English classics by reprinting in two dainty and artistically bound volumes those biting satires of Jonathan Swift, 'Gulliver's Travels.'"

IV—Tales from Irving. With illustrations. Two vols. Selected from "The Sketch Book," "Traveller," "Wolfert's Roost," "Bracebridge Hall." $2 00

" The tales, pathetic and thrilling as they are in themselves, are rendered winsome and realistic by the lifelike portraitures which profusely illustrate the volumes. . . . We confess our high appreciation of the superb manner in which the publishers have got up and sent forth the present volumes—which are real treasures, to be prized for their unique character."— *Christian Union.*

" Such books as these will find their popularity confined to no one country, but they must be received with enthusiasm wherever art and literature are recognized."—*Albany Argus.*

V—Book of British Ballads. Edited by S. C. HALL. A fac-simile of the original edition. With illustrations by CRESWICK, GILBERT, and others $1 50

" This is a diminutive fac-simile of the original very valuable edition. . . . The collection is not only the most complete and reliable that has been published, but the volume is beautifully illustrated by skilful artists."—*Pittsburg Chronicle.*

" Probably the best general collection of our ballad literature, in moderate compass, that has yet been made."—*Chicago Dial.*

VI—The Travels of Baron Münchausen. Reprinted from the early, complete edition. Very fully illustrated $1 25

" The venerable Baron Münchausen in his long life has never appeared as well-dressed, so far as we know, as now in this goodly company."

" The Baron's stories are as fascinating as the Arabian Nights."—*Church Union.*

VII—Letters, Sentences, and Maxims. By Lord CHESTERFIELD. With a critical essay by C. A. SAINTE-BEUVE $1 00

"Full of wise things, quaint things, witty and shrewd things, and the maker of this book has put the pick of them all together."—*London World.*

"Each of the little volumes in this series is a literary gem."—*Christian at Work.*

VIII—The Vicar of Wakefield. By GOLD-SMITH. With 32 illustrations by WILLIAM MUL-READY $1 00

"Goldsmith's charming tale seems more charming than ever in the dainty dress of the 'Knickerbocker Nuggets' series. These little books are a delight to the eye, and their convenient form and size make them most attractive to all book-lovers."—*The Writer*, Boston.

"A gem of an edition, well made, printed in clear, readable type, illustrated with spirit, and just such a booklet as, when one has it in his pocket, makes all the difference between solitude and loneliness."—*Independent.*

IX—Lays of Ancient Rome. By THOMAS BABINGTON MACAULAY. Illustrated by GEORGE SCHARF $1 00

"The poems included in this collection are too well known to require that attention should be drawn to them, but the beautiful setting which they receive in the dainty cover and fine workmanship of this series makes it a pleasure even to handle the volume."—*Yale Literary Magazine.*

X—The Rose and the Ring. By WILLIAM M. THACKERAY. With the author's illustrations. $1 25

"'The Rose and the Ring,' by Thackeray, is reproduced with quaint illustrations, evidently taken from the author's own handiwork."—*Rochester Post-Express.*

XI—Irish Melodies and Songs. By THOMAS MOORE. Illustrated by MACLISE . . $1 50

" The latest issue is a collection of Thomas Moore's ' Irish Melodies and Songs,' fully and excellently illustrated, with each page of the text printed within an outline border of appropriate green tint, embellished with emblems and figures fitting the text."—*Boston Times.*

XII—Undine and Sintram. By DE LA MOTTE FOUQUÉ. Illustrated $1 00

"' Undine and Sintram ' are the latest issue, bound in one volume. They are of the size classics should be—pocket volumes,—and nothing more desirable is to be found among the new editions of old treasures."—*San José Mercury.*

XIII—The Essays of Elia. By CHARLES LAMB. Two vols. $2 00

" The genial essayist himself could have dreamed of no more beautiful setting than the Putnams have given the *Essays of Elia* by printing them among their Knickerbocker Nuggets."—*Chicago Advance.*

XIV—Tales from the Italian Poets. By LEIGH HUNT. Two vols. . . . $2 00

. " The perfection of artistic bookmaking."—*San Francisco Chronicle.*

" This work is most delightful literature, which finds a fitting place in this collection, bound in volumes of striking beauty."— *Troy Times.*

" Hunt had just that delightful knowledge of the Italian poets that one would most desire for oneself, together with an exquisite style of his own wherein to make his presentation of them to English readers perfect."—*New York Critic.*

The first series, comprising the foregoing eighteen volumes, in handsome case, $19.00

XV.—Thoughts of the Emperor Marcus Aurelius Antoninus. Translated by GEORGE LONG $1 00

" The thoughts of the famous Roman are worthy of a new introduction to the army of readers through a volume so dainty and pleasing."—*Intelligencer.*

" As a book for hard study, as a book to inspire reverie, as a book for five minutes or an hour, it is both delightful and profitable."—*Journal of Education.*

" It is an interesting little book, and we feel indebted to the translator for this presentation of his work."—*Presbyterian.*

XVI.—Æsop's Fables. Rendered chiefly from original sources. By Rev. THOMAS JAMES, M.A. With 100 illustrations of JOHN TENNIELL . $1 25

" It is wonderful the hold these parables have had upon the human attention ; told to children, and yet of no less interest to men and women."—*Chautauqua Herald.*

" For many a long day nothing has been thought out or worked out so sure to prove entirely pleasing to cultured book-lovers."—*The Bookmaker.*

" These classic studies adorned with morals were never more neatly prepared for the public eye."—*The Milwaukee Wisconsin.*

XVII.—Ancient Spanish Ballads. Historic and Romantic. Translated, with notes, by J. G. LOCKHART. Reprinted from the revised edition of 1841, with 60 illustrations by ALLAN, ROBERTS, SIMSON, WARREN, AUBREY, and HARVEY . $1 50

" A mass of popular poetry which has never yet received the attention to which it is entitled."—*Boston Journal of Education.*

" The historical and artistic settings of these mediæval poetic gems enhance the value and attractiveness of the book."—*Buffalo Chronicle Advocate.*

XVIII.—**The Wit and Wisdom of Sydney Smith.** A selection of the most memorable passages in his Writings and Conversations . $1 00

" It is certainly a precious nugget that is presented in this issue, and the busy man of the world and the delving student will alike find occasion for blessing the compiler."—*Utica Herald.*

XIX.—**The Ideals of the Republic; or, Great Words from Great Americans.** Comprising:—" The Declaration of Independence, 1776." " The Constitution of the United States, 1779." " Washington's Circular Letter, 1783." " Washington's First Inaugural, 1789." " Washington's Second Inaugural, 1793." " Washington's Farewell Address." " Lincoln's First Inaugural, 1861." " Lincoln's Second Inaugural, 1865." " Lincoln's Gettysburg Address, 1863." . . $1 00

" Such a book ought to be in every American home. It ought to meet every immigrant to these shores. . . . They have never before been published in a form as convenient and elegant as that of this volume."—*Christian Intelligencer.*

XX.—**Selections from Thomas De Quincey.** Comprising:—" On Murder Considered as One of the Fine Arts." " Three Memorable Murders." " The Spanish Nun " $1 00

" Strangers to his works will find in this compilation a captivating introduction to them."—*Providence Journal.*

" All the delicacy of expression and felicity of arrangement familiar to the reader of De Quincey, appear here."—*Watertown Herald.*

G. P. PUTNAM'S SONS, PUBLISHERS
New York and London

www.ingramcontent.com/pod-product-compliance
Lightning Source LLC
Chambersburg PA
CBHW030324270326
41926CB00010B/1492